It's My Turn

FINDING IDENTITY AND PURPOSE AFTER THE EMPTY NEST

It's My Turn

Finding Identity and Purpose after The Empty Nest

JANINE HALL

authorHOUSE

AuthorHouse™
1663 Liberty Drive
Bloomington, IN 47403
www.authorhouse.com
Phone: 1 (800) 839-8640

© 2015 Janine Hall. All rights reserved.

No part of this book may be reproduced, stored in a retrieval system, or transmitted by any means without the written permission of the author.

Published by AuthorHouse 04/29/2015

ISBN: 978-1-4969-6413-7 (sc)
ISBN: 978-1-4969-6414-4 (e)

Library of Congress Control Number: 2015900444

Print information available on the last page.

Any people depicted in stock imagery provided by Thinkstock are models, and such images are being used for illustrative purposes only. Certain stock imagery © Thinkstock.

This book is printed on acid-free paper.

Because of the dynamic nature of the Internet, any web addresses or links contained in this book may have changed since publication and may no longer be valid. The views expressed in this work are solely those of the author and do not necessarily reflect the views of the publisher, and the publisher hereby disclaims any responsibility for them.

KJV
Scripture quotations marked KJV are from the Holy Bible, King James Version (Authorized Version). First published in 1611. Quoted from the KJV Classic Reference Bible, Copyright © 1983 by The Zondervan Corporation.

NIV
Scripture quotations marked NIV are taken from the Holy Bible, New International Version®. NIV®. Copyright © 1973, 1978, 1984 by International Bible Society. Used by permission of Zondervan. All rights reserved. [Biblica]

Contents

Foreword ix

The Empty Nest: Problems and Possibilities

Everyday Cake 1
The Sandwich Generation 4
Times of Transition 8
Recycling 12
Aging Women and the Workforce 16
The Middle-Aged Manifesto 19
Widowhood 23
Widow to Widow 26
Until Death Do Us Part 30
Caretakers 33

The Stress Mess

The Stress Mess 37
Stress Vulnerability Questionnaire 40

Anger—the Enemy Within 43
On the Go Again 47
Envy 49
Going Green 51
How Much Is Enough? 54
Identity Theft 57
Self-Defeating Ideas 59

Relationships

Seek First to Understand 65
Rx for Relationships 68
Interdependence 70
Synergy 72
Her Needs 74
His Needs 78
Men: Who Can Understand Them? 81
The Shelter of Each Other 83
The Battlefield 85
Pain Games 89

Christian Purpose-An Overview

Christian Purpose 95
Purposeful Living 97
Shaped for Serving God 100
Formed for God's Family 104
We Were Created to Become Like Christ 106
Mission Possible 109

Green and Growing: Personal Development

Identity 115
Self-Acceptance 118
Green and Growing... 122
Confidence.. 125
Contentment... 129
Creativity 132
Lights, Camera, Action 136
Uncovering a Multitude of Sins.. 139
Personal Management 142
Let God Be God 145
Risk... 147
Simplicity.. 150
Solitude... 153

Steps toward Serenity

Begin with the End in Mind 159
Differentiation 163
Myopia.. 165
Discomfort Dodging... 169
Feel Your Feelings 173
Your Coming-Out Party 176
Decisions, Decisions... 180
Three Boxes 183
Keep Your Eyes on Jesus 187
We All Have Choices 190
Bad Problems—Good Results.. 196
Tips to Reduce Stress 200
Write On...203

Overcoming Failure 207
Your Home as an Art Form 210
Move Your Muscles 213
A "Workin" 216
God—Our Greatest Supernatural Resource 218
The Least of These 222
Still Waters 225
Prayer 227

Foreword

We baby boomers are at or are approaching the third trimester of life. Our offspring have left home, and some of our children have children. We are peering into the future and thinking, *Now what?* The evenings sometimes get long, and we can spend time getting reacquainted with our spouses—because they are not the people they once were, and neither are we.

When children leave home, especially when it's the last one, parents may feel a loss of identity because their days of hands-on parenting are over. Women are especially prone to mourn this loss and can suffer from empty-nest syndrome. Single moms have already lost their significant others and may be hit especially hard when their children leave as well.

Retirement is here for some of us, or it is in the offing, and we have another big, nagging concern to face as we wonder how we will maintain our identities once our careers are over. How we will spend our time, and how will we handle being with our spouses for larger portions of the day?

We have more time for contemplation and spiritual things. We wonder how we fit into the big picture and the world around us. Change is often unsettling.

As we mature, we often come back to where we started. Although Carl Jung was not a Christian, his comment seems somewhat appropriate: "Your vision becomes clear only when you look into your own heart. Who looks outside dreams; who looks inside awakes."

If the Holy Spirit lives inside you, He will help and guide you as you look for purpose after your children leave you with an empty nest.

This book tries to define the challenges of this new stage in life, outline helpful skills and attitudes to help achieve a more successful life adjustment, and give you practical and godly ideas to help you experience more serenity in this crazy, chaotic existence we call modern life.

There are as many purposes for living as there are people. It is by design that you are like no other. It is no accident that you are exactly where you are at this particular time in history. God created us all for a purpose. We need to ask God to help us discover why He put us here and then be willing to accept our assignments.

The Empty Nest: Problems and Possibilities

Everyday Cake

When I was a young girl, my mom baked several kinds of cakes. Chocolate cake with chocolate frosting was our favorite, and because we loved it, we often ate too much. But most of the time, my mom made an everyday cake—a yellow cake with no frosting.

Everyday cake provided us with a rest from our labors and some conversation about the issues of the day. Eating it was less memorable than eating chocolate cake, but it answered our need to have something warm in our stomachs and to enjoy a repast with each other. Underneath the accomplishments of our everyday routine, one could sense "the song of the family" while the parameters of our daily tasks formed our family identity.

The commonality of nearly every woman's life is to bake the everyday cake for her family. Much of our self-esteem comes from the knowledge that we have done the daily repeated tasks necessary to provide a sustaining sense of permanence for our families. Doing the dishes, the laundry, or taking out the trash are not very glamorous jobs, but they are essential and instrumental in creating a pleasant and cohesive home environment.

When we heard the "song of the family" playing in the background, it was a safe assumption that our mothers were around. Motherhood is a privilege and is the most important job on earth.

In addition to caring for our children, we must care for the little boy that lives inside our husband, if we have one. Being a mom to all our children, big and little, is an experience that almost all women have as a common source of connection because most of us have "been there, done that."

It's the small increments of daily tasks that shape our lives. They are the basic ingredients of the everyday cake that feeds both the body and the spirit of most people on the planet. When we walk the dog, make a meal, read a book to the children, or sweep the kitchen floor, we are adding ingredients to the most basic dish for the most important group on earth—the human family.

Our special talents, no matter how well hidden, our career skills, our gifts of time to our families and friends, our individual accomplishments, and our areas of interest are the icing on the cake in the form of service to others. Some of us are disgruntled because we are cream cheese frosting when we always wanted to be chocolate. We have to accept what we are and are not. Shakespeare's sister lives within all of us because she did the dishes and put her children to bed.

All of our contributions are equal in the sight of the Lord. We are to consider each other's accomplishments and talents greater than our own. Everyone has a story to tell or a message to give. A kind heart and genuine helpfulness are gifts from God.

The Bible says we all have promises and possibilities hidden inside us that can benefit the group, and it is our duty to unearth them. But the more essential, the most needed, and the most significant accomplishment we all can have is to bake the everyday cake for our families. Sometimes we feel that we did not follow the recipe very well or left out a major ingredient, or we wish we had done a better job. We need to remember to pray every day for our families and remember that when we do the best we can, God will do the rest.

> No people ever rise higher than to the point to which they elevate their women.
>
> —Isobella Thorburn

The Sandwich Generation

～❧～

Often, middle-aged women find themselves giving time, energy, and money to their children as well as to their aging parents. Teenagers and college-age students have expensive needs, and the downturn in the economy puts added financial stress on the rite-of-passage generation and their parents.

As life-expectancy ages increase, the middle generation tends to have parents that survive into advanced age. The number of children in a family is decreasing, so there are fewer siblings to share the burden of caring for aging parents. Due to greater mobility, the demographics draw a picture of greater distances between the location of one generation and another, which makes the process of making decisions about caregiving more complicated and disrupted.

Middle-aged women often spend a considerable amount of time helping their elderly parents with errands and personal care and providing them with financial assistance, as well as helping to support the young adults in their nuclear families, even if they no longer reside at home. The depressed job market and the rising cost of living make it hard for young people just starting out to keep their financial boats afloat. College tuition has increased so much that a college education is unattainable for many people, and school debt has crippled the ability of many young people to get a grip on their financial future. Large numbers of the fledging youth return to the nest.

In former years, women were not involved in the workforce as much as they are now, and they had more time and energy to devote to accommodating the needs of their aging parents and their own children who were preparing to start out on their own. They were more logistically able to tend to the tasks of guiding their children's transition from childhood into becoming responsible adults. Now it is necessary that women work to make both ends meet, so tending to the needs of the generation before them and the generation after them has become very burdensome.

It is not common for women in this age group to be living with both their parents and their children, but it is common for them to be supporting their children and their parents simultaneously in less-dramatic ways.

This middle-aged group, squeezed between aging parents and dependent offspring, is known as the sandwich generation. This delicate balancing act is a familiar one in far more Americans homes than you might expect. An estimated sixteen million American families fall into this category, which is more people than live in all of the states of New England.

Janine Hall

As we look down the road, the number of families affected is about to explode. In twenty-five years, there will be sixty million Americans between the ages of sixty-six and eighty-four, many of whom will need part- or full-time care.

Midlife brings with it not only the problems of people adjusting to the needs of their and their coming-of-age children, but also of adapting to the changing roles that accompany this stage. These changes require flexibility and the ability to respond well to new situations. We need to slowly let go of our children as they approach adulthood. And conversely, we must assume a parental role in caring for our elderly parents.

It seems evident that middle-aged women are saddled with too much responsibility and not enough time to keep the bases covered. The statistics show that their assisting their children is a more capital-intensive activity, while assisting their parents is generally more labor-intensive in nature. In addition, a sizable group of middle-age women spend an average of twenty-eight hours a week providing childcare for their grandchildren while their own children work or attend school.

The astronomical price tag of nursing-home care is causing many children of aging parents to look for alternative solutions to their parents' healthcare needs. The Area Agency of Aging strives to keep seniors in their homes as long as possible. Agencies like Respite Care and Home Instead give much-needed breaks to caregivers.

If adult children aren't able to escort their parents on shopping trips or other important events and help them with daily tasks, they look for alternative caregivers. Senior centers, The Meals on Wheels Association of America, Home Health, and agencies that help with housekeeping and supply companionship are very valuable to the well-being of seniors who reside in their own homes and give added peace of mind to their adult children.

The group of middle-aged women represented in the article reported that an average of $10,000 and 1,350 hours annually are spent helping their children and their parents. The troublesome situation about elder care opens up an area of future career options for those looking for employment.

The Japanese symbol for *crisis* is also the symbol for *opportunity*. It seems that new problems and situations are often resolved, but it takes time for society to work them out. There is a bright future for those who will come up with new and workable solutions for appropriate and affordable elder care that is desirable to the seniors and helps middle-aged women to balance the load of their responsibilities.

References:

CBS News Video

The Lifespan by Guy R. Lefrancois

The

By Charles R. Pierret

Sandwich Generation: Caring for Parents and Children—A Longitudinal Survey

Times of Transition

⚜

Somewhere in the middle years of our lives, there is a change in our perception of time. Middle age is the autumn of our lives, and it is clear that the spring and summer are gone. We realize we have more yesterdays than we have tomorrows. Our youthful feelings of immortality and invulnerability may be starting to crumble. This shift in attitude is thought to occur approximately from age forty-five to about sixty or sixty-five.

There are important developmental tasks to complete in this stage in order to age successfully. These new criteria largely consist of generativity versus self-absorption as well as maintaining satisfying social relationships and mental and emotional flexibility.

With increasing maturity, the adult needs to maintain or establish work and other activities that are beneficial to the world and the community—that is, to be productive rather than to become absorbed in the self. Of course, the resolution of these requirements doesn't call for a complete abandonment of thoughts about ourselves, but rather, it helps us establish a balance between our self-interests and the interests of others.

In this stage of life, women become more aggressive and men begin to mellow. Some experts believe that this happens because the polarized sex roles required for raising children relax and blend into similar outlooks and behavior.

As we expend our energies, our activities should mean more to us than being ways to make a living or merely ways to kill time. Our occupations should provide a means of self-discovery and self-expression that give us a sense of contribution to our families and to society. We need to do things that give us a sense of fulfillment and purpose.

A common way to express generativity is through our families. Grandparenting is an excellent way to contribute and give back. We can do those things that young parents don't have the time or the money to do. If you have molded a child, you have changed the world.

Although motherhood is the most important job on earth, putting all our proverbial eggs in the "mommy basket" can leave us searching for a modicum of identity and purpose after the children leave home. Now we can shift our emphasis from raising children to serving others outside our nuclear family. There is so much good in life that needs to be done, so find ways to put your shoulder to the wheel.

Middle age often results in changes in our relationships from an emphasis on sexuality and sexual behavior to friendship, trust, emotional and moral support, and companionship.

Janine Hall

Competition and an emphasis on impressive careers and material possessions often give way to connections with others and cooperation for the common good. In midlife, satisfying relationships play a large role in quality life experiences.

Social as well as physical adjustments require adaption and change. Many of our emotional ties may be strained or severed for a variety of reasons. At this stage of life, people die, children leave home, couples divorce, and careers end. We will need to form new relationships and oftentimes forget others. We must be able to find support and give it as well.

Flexibility and the ability to rebound from setbacks, as well as the willingness to learn new things, contribute to the viability of the midlife experience. Cultural changes require us to deal with new ideas. Regular spiritual nourishment helps us discern whether to accept or reject societal change. Society advances, and to a certain degree, we need to advance with it. It is the sign of being a good captain when you are able to change course in light of new information.

Keeping fit is proactive in preventing physical and mental diseases that are sometimes associated with the onset of later adulthood. Walking and regular aerobic exercise can prevent obesity and all its accompanying negative effects to our health, such as high blood pressure, heart disease, strokes, and some kinds of cancer. Health problems make it hard to maintain quality of life.

At the end of this transition bridging middle adulthood to late adulthood, the key tasks will be reconciling your life's dreams with reality, accepting the notion of your own mortality, and preparing for the radical changes brought about by retirement.

Many people aren't aware that there are stages of adulthood and that there are developmental tasks that accompany them. Knowledge is power, and it is good to read and stay informed in order to be abreast of new criteria that we will need to meet in order to age successfully.

Recycling

A few years ago, Bill Clinton said "When you get to my age, you've had more yesterdays than you will have tomorrows." As aging baby boomers we will enjoy unprecedented longevity because of improved health care and safer living conditions. We are the "young" old and we are entering Into the third trimester of life.

As we stand on the cusp of time and peer into our tomorrows, we women with empty nests discover that we will need to reinvent ourselves in order to find new purpose and new productivity. Our children may now have children and we are looking for a new lease on life.

We need to
>renew,
>reestablish,
>rejuvenate,
>and redefine ourselves.

Our mothers drew their identity from their husbands. We have had more educational opportunities, more financial resources and more lifestyle choices.

The average life expectancy for a woman at this time is eighty years old. Sixty is the new forty. We are much "younger" and more vital than our mother's generation and we have more options.

As a result of having more choices and opportunities, we also experience more ambivalence and anxiety because we experience gender confusion. There are no longer any clear cut and well clarified definitions of the woman's role in society. Women's lifestyles vary considerably and it is a rare person who can do it all.

When choosing our lifestyle, our best game plan is to dish up our specialties and then do our best to promote respect between all women who have differing career paths or walks of life.

A speaker I heard recently said if we live to be sixty the odds are very good that we will live to be ninety. In their book A Time of Their Own, Greenburg and Whitney identified the qualities that enhance one's likelihood of longevity. They are as follows: optimism, good genetics, adapting to a changing family structure, hard work, eating simply, faith, a connection with nature and a sense of humor.

Whitney and Greenburg report that at the present time in America only one third of women in their late fifties and sixties turn to faith for meaning and comfort. That is very sad. But almost all women in this category become more reflective and introspective searching for spiritual meaning and significance. Perhaps this is because we have more time to devote to contemplation.

Most women entering the third trimester of life are employed to some degree, are relatively healthy and are intertwined in relationships with their husbands and other significant people in their lives. Many of our contemporaries have a few close alliances with other women as opposed to many casual acquaintances and friends.

The biggest elemental change for this age group is the advent of grand parenting. This welcomenew role often influences how we spend our nonworking hours and where we spend our vacations. Some women begin to whittle down their community responsibilities in order to spend more time with their burgeoning families as they fill the role of matriarch in the family structure.

As the family structure changes, the middle-aged woman needs to be flexible enough to change with it. Our personalities need to be more like plastic than like plaster. We must learn to go with the flow and allow our children to lead their own lives.

During this stage, some marriages feel stale and some women experience a great deal of restlessness. But conversely, some couples in this age group rediscover the happiness of their early years. Perhaps this is due to the slower pace, fewer responsibilities and more quiet times of togetherness.

Each woman brings to the third trimester a lifetime of adapting and learning within her family, her work life and her social environment. As we move from one life stage to another, we must redefine ourselves and use our set of skills in new ways in order to live life to the fullest. For many, the third trimester is a time of increased freedom and an opportunity to choose one's own activities. It truly can be a time our own.

This essay contains information from the book A Time of Her Own by Elinor Greenberg and Fay Wadsworth Whitney

Aging Women and the Workforce

The baby boomer generation has had an incredible impact on the workforce. We are the first generation to be largely employed outside the home. Satisfactory work performance and a meaningful job description give any worker a sense of identity and usefulness. As female workers age, they can provide younger workers with a "mother figure" in the workplace. But from middle age to retirement, there are common problems for female workers for a variety of reasons.

These issues are: ageism, a diminishing ability to adapt to job stress, changing technology, sexual harassment, unemployment, and adjustment to retirement.

Although older workers are usually reliable and have a strong work ethic, they are sometimes seen as inflexible. It is difficult to keep abreast of new skills and job requirements. Some older women find that their job skills are outdated or no longer in demand.

Some aging workers just run out of gas and find it difficult to stand up to the regimen of caring for the home and working forty hours a week. Responding to this challenge is demanding at any age. Part-time employment becomes attractive to many aging women.

Because of political correctness, working relationships between male and female employees can be awkward. But if sexual harassment is actually occurring, a woman doesn't know if she will be believed, or she may fear embarrassment, hostility, or losing her job.

Too much stress at work can cause physical, mental, or psychological problems. Stress in the workplace can cause cardiac problems or difficulties such as anxiety or depression. Contributing factors can be excessive job demands, negative patterns of supervision and communication, or lack of respect or recognition.

Although employers may not admit they would rather hire younger job applicants, ageism is a factor. Companies, school systems, and government agencies often don't want to employ older workers because they don't want to pay for their years of experience.

Sometimes, instead of providing costly and extensive training to older, existing workers, it's more expedient to hire younger workers who already have the necessary training and are more flexible and adaptable to change. This is especially true in jobs with technological aspects.

Since the economic turndown, unemployment has been a chronic problem, and older workers face discrimination when it comes to rehiring. Many companies offer to "buy out" older workers by offering them retirement package. Many of these "buyouts" offer too little compensation for the older employee's years of service, but there is little choice in the matter.

It's not only men who choose to work part-time to help fill retired life with a sense of purpose or extra money to supplement social security or retirement pensions. Women who have always worked or are not very domestic may need the identity that work provides or the structure it lends to their lives. Many widows are suddenly faced with the need to find a job to help support themselves.

All things considered, it's a tremendous accomplishment for a woman to maintain a job and a home through a lengthy career. When they retire, they can pat themselves on the back for a job well done. But the fact remains that aging workers often face problems that younger women don't have to grapple with.

The Middle-Aged Manifesto

Curves, an exercise business, does not allow customers to exercise twice on the same day. The reasoning behind this directive is because your muscles need time to adjust to the effects of aerobic exercise.

Our minds need time to accommodate and assimilate new information and to modify our viewpoints, if necessary. When our lives are bombarded with massive amounts of information and wall-to-wall people and problematic situations from sun up to sun down, our inner equilibrium is thrown off balance. We feel like a washing machine that is noisily shaking out of control, and we think, *Stop the world; I want to get off*—at least for a while.

On the evening news, it was said that the most stressed group of people on the planet are middle-aged women. Women wear too many hats and are spread too thin, and they don't have any time to call their own.

A middle-aged woman must contend with her teenagers or college-age students that are a big source of stress and a big drain on the checkbook. Because of the current recession, many adult children return to the nest because they cannot find jobs or make enough money to support themselves.

Most middle-aged women are working full-time and are trying to balance career and family with little time left over to maintain their marriages. Many of them belong to the sandwich generation and are juggling their children's needs with the needs of their aging parents. No wonder they are the most burnt-out segment of the population and that more than half of all marriages fail.

Middle-aged women need people in their lives to care about their needs and to help them bear their burdens as well. They need to get support from their husbands and their children. Call a family meeting and deliver the "middle-aged manifesto" to state that you have needs too and that you need their cooperation.

First, you should tell your youngsters that they can only be in one activity. Because of hard economic times, they should find jobs, if at all possible, to help bear the financial burden of purchasing the things they need. That would be a far better experience to teach them life skills than dance or karate.

You must muster up the courage to ask your mate to assume more of the tasks at home. You also need to pencil in some solitude in your schedule to de-stress and read the Bible or other reading material that you enjoy—whatever it is that you like to do as therapy for dealing with the problems of your day.

You are not shirking your responsibilities if you are not involved in community service. There will plenty time for that after the children leave home.

No amount of worldly success and community honors can compensate for failure on the home front.

Divorce shatters lives and usually creates instant poverty for all that are involved. It seems that some of it could be avoided if the marriage partners had their priorities straight and realized that divorce is often an exchange of one set of problems for another set of problems. There are going to be times when you don't like your spouse or when things are a bit dysfunctional. Sometimes, divorce it is the only option that makes sense, but we all need to examine our expectations and realize that there is no perfect marriage.

God designed you to need Him and to need others. We have missed the whole point of our existence if we are trying to achieve status and are striving to collect and catalog our success symbols. If you don't have time for relationships, you are too busy.

When our personal lives are spent on too many activities with little or no direction, we need to rethink what is essential and what can be eliminated from the schedule. Have that family meeting and decide just what it is that you want to accomplish at home. Tell your family you don't have a big, red superwoman cape and that they should cut you some slack. Create your own "middle-aged manifesto," and tell your family you are only one person.

Janine Hall

Each woman is far from average in the daily heroics of her life, even though she may never receive a moment's recognition in history.

—"Women and Work," *Newsage Press*

Widowhood

At the present time, there is a much higher percentage of widows than widowers. In his book *Lifespan*, R. Lefrancois attributes this to the fragility of the male.

Traditionally, males were under more stress because they were the breadwinners. But recently, sources report that females are beginning to die at younger ages because of the stress-load they bear by both maintaining a job in the workforce and taking the lead in maintaining the home front and caring for the children.

In 1999, there were 50 percent more women than men at the age of sixty-five. The ratio becomes increasingly more unbalanced as age levels advance. In 1995, there were 8.6 million widows above the age of sixty-four but only 1.8 million widowers in the same age range. The gap between these two groups has probably narrowed somewhat for the aforementioned reason, but it's likely that remarriage is not an option for many older single women. Our society doesn't prepare us for widowhood. It is something we don't want to think about.

We have a very sketchy sense of our own mortality and especially that of our mates. The relative good health of young people allows them to think that death is too far in the future to give it much consideration. Until people our own age begin to pass away, we all feel ten feet tall and bulletproof. But when we, or people who are close to us, face serious illnesses that threaten life, our perspective changes.

Some researchers say that widowhood is harder the younger women are when their mate dies. Supposedly, older women are more financially stable than they were in their youth. Certainly, coping with grief combined with the prospect of raising young children alone would be devastating.

One of the relatively common outcomes of losing a spouse is depression. However, in most cases, it is short-lived. Loneliness can be a more long-term factor, but widows are better than widowers in banding together with those in the same situation.

Women who lose their mates have to redefine their sense of self and find a new normal. The bonds of matrimony and the threads of common experience connect us at such deep levels that we feel that a big part of us is missing when death parts us from our spouse. We need to recover from our grief before we can begin to engage in the personal growth that is required to feel whole again.

After the grieving period, most widows find social outlets with their old friends and usually make new friends with women who are widows themselves.

To gain their equilibrium, widows put more energy in their families, their work, or social organizations and causes. For some, remarriage is the answer. With the passage of time, most widows make a good adjustment and become happy, productive citizens.

Widow to Widow

~❦~

Genevieve Ginsberg, who is a widow herself, begins her book *Widow to Widow* by stating, "Each year more than a million people will join the 13.8 million widows and widowers in the United States. Yet each time it happens it is an uniquely individual sorrow as though it never happened before."

Another widow friend said to me, "Before I became a widow myself, I had no idea what women in our situation were going through."

There is truth to both statements. Experience is the best teacher. Whether you live intimately or not so intimately with a spouse for a long period of time, you are knitted together by the threads of common experience and many complicated marital-relational patterns.

The severance of the marriage relationship leaves you feeling that a part of you has just been amputated. Shock numbs the pain, and other people may think you are doing well. It is denial that is enabling you to function while you are trying on a new role and trying to answer the age-old question, "Who am I?" in a whole new and elusive way.

There are no words to describe the first few weeks of widowhood. You have to have been there to understand. I found watching Christian television to be very helpful.

Sleeping and eating patterns are disrupted. More normal eating habits usually return relatively quickly, but your sleeping patterns may not return to normal until the first year or so is over. Some people with multiple losses in a short period of time may never regain the ability to sleep through the entire night.

Greif is said to come in waves. Just when you think you are getting your bearings, another tsunami comes your way, like the aftershocks of an earthquake.

The ebb and flow is just natural, but sometimes something reminds you of your spouse and you go down for the count. I went to my husband's place of work a few months after he passed away, and that was a big mistake.

Dealing with the deluge of paperwork from banks, insurance companies, social security, mortuaries, retirement accounts, the Veteran's Administration, and a myriad of other entities becomes your part-time job. Many of them need death certificates from the state department and other pertinent information.

Janine Hall

All this busy work floods your life at the time when you become solely responsible for performing every private task and public responsibility the two of you once shared.

Every widow seems to have a hair-raising story about the little or not-so-little emergencies that occurred in the first year of sailing the stormy seas of single life. Mine was no different.

Couple friends don't come around anymore, and you find yourself seeking the shelter of your old women friends. The entrance requirements for the social club called widowhood are not ones women want to have happen, but one feels drawn to others experiencing the same situation. Many of the members at the local senior center are widows, and it has become a real answer for me.

Early on, a no-cost grief group put on by the local hospital helped me to realize that the difficulties I was experiencing were normal, that no one else was bouncing back immediately, and that these things take time. Widows should be supportive of one another, but comparisons should be avoided because every situation is different and everyone grieves in his or her own way.

Grief is as individual and unique as the person who is experiencing it. It differs according to age, the nature of the relationship, family and social support, financial considerations, spiritual resources, and the personality and mental health of the new widow.

If someone doesn't put copies of good books about grieving and widowhood into your hands shortly after your husband dies, go directly to the bookstore and purchase some. I was fortunate enough to get some books on grieving from my pastor, and a relative gave me a copy of *Widow to Widow* almost immediately.

Widowhood is a bit like retirement in that there is no way to fully understand what it is going to be like until you get there. It is a big bump in the road, and you will never be the same as you were before it happened. Grieving is a process rather than a series of uphill steps, and gains are most often realized in retrospect.

Until Death Do Us Part

Just as you don't know what it is like to be married or retired until you experience it, losing your mate is a dark unknown, and each of us responds like it was the first time it ever happened to anyone. Shortly after I was widowed, another recently widowed friend commented, "I had no idea what women in our position were going through until now." Because situations are diverse and because of an entire gamut of individual differences, every woman reacts differently to the bereavement of losing her husband. This is how it was for me in the early stages.

My husband died yesterday, and I'm sitting in my recliner in an empty house in the dark. The 24-7, round-the-clock care is over, and now I am lost in nothingness. I feel impaled on the moment, and I cannot think or feel.

Time seems to stand still. I think that only an hour must have passed, but when I look at the clock, I cannot believe that actually four or six hours have gone by. Life is moving in freeze-frames instead of reel to reel.

I knew it was coming but the finality of it has hit me like the slamming of a prison cell door. I want to remain here in the cell until I can begin to comprehend the enormity of the event that has just transpired.

His death is like a doorway into a dark, dark place where a heavy curtain of denial prevents me from experiencing the reality of the pain of separation that has just ripped our lives apart like two stubs of a movie ticket to a show I don't want to see. I'm in the epicenter of the drama, and there's no stopping it.

Part of me is gone—torn away by the roadside bomb that ended our relationship and put us on opposite sides of eternity. I'm trying to take stock of my injuries, and I realize that I no longer know who I am. How will I present myself to the world, and what will my new normal be? The pain and shock of widowhood surrounds me and separates me from the rest of society.

Then another bomb shakes my life only four months later, when my father dies. It so complicates things that I feel it will take years to resolve my grief and distinguish one from the other. Now I am fatherless as well.

As a year passes, I am functioning and doing things, but I feel dead on the inside. I wonder if spring will ever come to the frozen wasteland inside my soul.

Janine Hall

One day, I feel that God is telling me to come out of myself. A television minister seems to be calling to me personally. He says, "You do not have a past, you only have a future."

I immediately come out of my stupor in a process very similar to being born again. I start looking forward instead of looking backward, and soon I begin experiencing what God had up His sleeve for me in the future.

I am not the same person I was in the past. I am an individual in my own right, and a new normal is beginning to unfold. That fateful day seems long ago and far away. It's a place I don't want revisit very often, because there will always be a hole in my heart where my marriage used to be.

Caretakers

Many people prefer to be at home during long recuperations from serious health problems or to remain at home for as long as they can when suffering from terminal illnesses. Patients feel more secure and more comfortable in their home environments, and most people want to avoid the ever-increasing cost of nursing-home stays.

The quality of care for the patient is the first priority, but care and consideration should be given to the caretaker as well. Caregivers need breaks from the constant stress they are under, and the companionship of friends and family is needed therapy. Hospice and other related organizations provide time for the caregiver to do needed business or to find relief from the pressures of the twenty-four-hour responsibility they are shouldering.

This list of signs of caretaker stress is put out by the Alzheimer's Association, but they are applicable to caregivers who must stand up to the demands of acute care for any disease or chronic condition.

- Denial about the disease and its effects on the person who has been diagnosed. "I know Mom's going to get better."
- Anger at the person with the disease or anger that no cure exists. Also anger that people don't understand what's happening. "If he asks me that question one more time, I am going to scream!"
- Social withdrawal from friends and activities that once brought pleasure. "I don't care about getting together with the neighbors anymore."
- Anxiety about the future. "What happens when he needs more care than I can provide?"
- Depression that breaks your spirit and affects your ability to cope. "I don't care anymore."
- Exhaustion that makes it nearly impossible to complete necessary daily tasks. "I'm too tired for this."
- Sleeplessness caused by a never-ending list of concerns. "What if she wanders away or falls and hurts herself?"
- Irritability that leads to moodiness and triggers negative responses and reactions. "Leave me alone."
- Lack of concentration that makes it difficult to perform familiar tasks. "I was so busy, I forgot we had an appointment."
- Health problems that begin to take a mental and physical toll. "I can't remember the last time I felt good."

If you have family or friends living under these circumstances, anything you can do for either the patient or the caregiver is doing something for the both of them and is you being the hands and feet of Jesus.

The Stress Mess

The Stress Mess

Stress is a normal part of life and everybody experiences it. Stress is your body's reaction to demands, events, and changes. Both positive and negative experiences can create stress. Stress can be a motivator, but too much stress for too long a period of time can affect your physical and emotional well-being. Like capping the massive BP oil leak in the gulf, we need to control our stress at its source before it pollutes our system and overwhelms us.

When you're stressed, your heart pumps faster, your breathing speeds up, and your body produces fight-or-flight hormones that cause you to feel edgy or tense.

Stress plays a role in heart attacks, accidents, lung disease, liver disease, depression, ulcers, and anxiety. As many as 70 percent of all doctor's visits are related to stress.

Exercise is a great stress reducer. Exercise is a form of controlled, predictable stress that is a vaccination against uncontrollable, unavoidable stress that leads to physical illness, depression, or anxiety. Activity that raises the heart rate is ideal, but walking, dancing, or participating in sports is helpful as well. Yoga, meditation, or Tai chi can help us to de-stress.

Your diet can help your body to avoid stress. Coffee and other caffeinated drinks can put you on edge. Eating good, nourishing foods helps your body to perform well and can give you the endurance you need to deal with the daily stressors that are an unavoidable part of life. A good night's sleep can do wonders.

We need to train ourselves to drop out of the rat race on a regular basis to indulge in some quietude where relaxation, rejuvenation, and healing can take place. Donna Carter, in her book *10 Smart Things Women Can Do to Build a Better Life,* urges us to "give ourselves permission not to do it all."

Taking time to pray and to read the Bible and other Christian materials has a powerful positive impact on the human psyche. Spiritual growth helps us to stay in the eye of the storm and gives our lives purpose and meaning. Faith is contagious and it can be "caught" in the fellowship of believers.

God's presence in our lives is the best tranquilizer available to calm the storms of life, and His services are free. Being dependent on God is the only habitual crutch that can set you free instead of enslaving you.

Karla Domacher has constructed an impressive list of good reasons to seek out a relationship with God. She said, "I will not forget the benefits of knowing God: Unconditional love. Forgiveness of sins. Eternal salvation. A second chance. Peace beyond understanding. Truth that sets me free. Protection from evil one. My daily bread. The joy of the Lord. And so much more."

It is a widely accepted premise that persons of faith handle stress better than those who feel no connection with God. When we start to miss sleep, meals, breaks from stress, time with our family and friends, and time with God, we start to sink. Children are not the only ones that need a schedule. Healthy routines help make us strong enough to withstand the firestorms of life. Schedule some serenity into each day.

Contains some ideas from the book *10 Smart Things Women Can Do to Build a Better Life* by Donna Carter

Stress Vulnerability Questionnaire

⚜

Read each statement carefully, and reflect upon your typical behaviors. Then write the appropriate number indicating how often the statement applies to you using the following scale.

Always—1

Most of the time—2

Sometimes—3

Almost never—4

Never—5

1._____I eat at least one hot, balanced meal a day.
2._____I get seven to eight hours of sleep at least four nights a week.
3._____I give and receive affection regularly.
4._____I have at least one relative within fifty miles on whom I can rely.

5. _____ I exercise to the point of perspiration at least twice a week.
6. _____ I smoke less than half a pack of cigarettes a day.
7. _____ I take fewer than five alcoholic drinks per week.
8. _____ I have an income adequate to meet my basic needs.
9. _____ I am the appropriate weight for my height.
10. _____ I get strength from my religious beliefs.
11. _____ I regularly attend club or social activities.
12. _____ I have a network of close friends and acquaintances.
13. _____ I have one or more friends to confide in about personal matters.
14. _____ I am able to speak openly about my feelings when I am angry or worried.
15. _____ I have regular conversations with the people I live with about domestic problems such as chores, money, and daily living needs.
16. _____ I do something for fun at least once a week.
17. _____ I am able to organize my time effectively.
18. _____ I drink fewer that three cups of coffee (or tea or cola) a day.
19. _____ I take quiet time for myself during the day.
20. _____ I am in good health, including eyesight, hearing, dental health, etc.

Now add up your scores for each statement. Scores will range from 20 to 100. If your score is less than 50, you are not vulnerable to stress at this time. Any score over 50 indicates vulnerability to stress. Evaluate the reasons for the stress, and identify strategies for dealing with it. Periodically monitor your progress toward reducing stress.

A score between 70 and 95 indicates a serious vulnerability toward reducing stress. Drastic lifestyle changes may be necessary to avoid the detrimental effects of stress. A score over 95 indicates extreme vulnerability to stress. Intervention and assistance from outside sources, such as counselors, may be necessary. http://alc.stcloud.edu/Counseling/CLASSES

Anger—the Enemy Within

Anger and hostility can disfigure a life and make peace of mind an impossibility.

Conditions and situations that can lead to anger include insecurity, a feeling of being controlled in a job setting or in a relationship, or being hurt by others in our lives.

Anger opens the door for Satan to control us and to prevent blessings from unfolding in our lives. He's delighted to see us fuss and stew. Satan's supreme goal is to keep us from experiencing the peace and satisfaction of a right relationship with Jesus Christ.

If this area is a problem for you, ask God to increase your awareness of the ways in which Satan is trying to fan the flames of your thought life. Also ask for protection from his whole arsenal of anger-enhancing weapons. If you want to brush up on the spiritual warfare that is going on all around you, the book *Everyone's Guide to Demons and*

Spiritual Warfare by Ron Phillips provides instruction on biblical and commonsense tools to use to fight our enemy.

We need to determine whether our anger has its source in old wounds or if it is a result of a situation developing at the present time—or a combination of both. This process isn't pleasant or easy, but you can't put out a forest fire if you are in the wrong neck of the woods. God knows exactly what's going on, so ask Him for discernment.

Submerging our anger or compartmentalizing it beneath the surface keeps it out of sight for a while, but if it is not resolved, it results in physical or mental problems and renders us less effective.

People in general, and women in particular, have real problems with jealousy. If we can learn to recognize it as such, it will help us not to act upon our envy in negative ways.

We are to love God above all others. Our relationship with Him is more important than our relationships with our husbands, our children, and our friends.

Pleasing Him and obeying Him is the worship He seeks. In Ephesians 4:26, we find God's advice: "When angry do not sin and do not let your wrath last until the sun goes down." That's a tall order, but obedience brings many benefits.

Finding effective and constructive ways to control our tempers is very important. It is an excellent extra benefit of physical exercise. Venting angry emotions in a journal is helpful for some people. Approaching

God in prayer allows the Holy Spirit to minister to us and neutralize and soothe our upset feelings to bring us peace.

Avoiding replaying upsetting events from the past allows these events to run their course and lose their power over us. Talking to people from our pasts and giving and receiving forgiveness can be very healing. The Bible says if we sow mercy and *forgiveness*, we will find them.

Forgiveness is an atomic power that results in peace of mind. Many of us think that there are some things we cannot forgive. But with God's help, situations can look remarkably different. When we enter into prayer expecting progress, we can take giant strides toward wholeness.

Victory over the self is always sweet and is often a prerequisite to blessings.

"Better a patient man than a warrior, a man who controls his temper than one who takes a city."

Joyce Meyer tells us that we need to learn to get angry without sinning. How very hard to do. If we can exercise self-control in this way, we can actually allow what is causing us to be angry to build godly character within us. Pray about it to get spiritual stamina and strength. Leave no foothold for Satan to pry into your life and tempt you to strike out onto the source of your injury or provocation. This is a hard area for me.

Unresolved anger and resentments are a ball and chain preventing us from becoming more like Christ. Some situations that make us angry were sent by God as a test of our faith or are trials by fire that enable God to change or purify us.

Satan enjoys making us angry and sends barbs and arrows intended to inflame our tempers in order to prevent us from experiencing God's love and faithfulness. If anger is a reoccurring problem for us, we need to quench our flames of anger by searching for biblical solutions, going to see our pastor or a Christian counselor, and approaching God in prayer to find rest and peace. Venting angry emotions in a journal is helpful for some people. The Holy Spirit can come to us and neutralize and dissipate our anger. The persons who will most benefit by forgiving others is ourselves.

It's easy to coddle our feelings and nurse our hurts. But when we forgive, we take giant strides toward wholeness. God does not stay angry at us, so He expects us not to stay angry with others. We need to ask Him to help us to learn to forgive others and lose our desire to get back at those who hurt us. Proverbs 14:17a reads, "A quick tempered man does foolish things." The Bible also says that if we sow forgiveness and mercy, we will obtain them.

Finding effective and constructive ways to control our tempers is very important.

The following verse illustrates the huge advantage of controlling anger: "Better a patient man than a warrior, a man who controls his temper than one who takes a city" (Proverbs 16:32).

On the Go Again

At the present time, our society dictates that the one with the longest list of activities wins. Many of us are over-employed by necessity, but some of us think we are not doing enough for the community, so we take on another responsibility. We have become human "doings" instead of human beings.

Many middle-aged women are working extra jobs to make ends meet. Some are financially assisting their adult children who cannot find suitable work, are struggling with divorce, or can't deal with rising prices and underemployment. The poor economy and the tumult and terror of the world situation affects us all.

Although we know and accept that idleness is the devil's workshop, our breakneck speed anesthetizes our life experiences with stress, enables us to avoid our issues, leaves unfulfilled the roles we were meant to play, and leave us spiritually impoverished because we have no time to talk to God and search for meaning in our lives.

We need to be more contemplative, and I know that's easier said than done for many of us. Understanding what has happened in our past, realizing what is happening to us now, and looking into the future to determine what may happen then lends some continuity to life. Perhaps some problems can be prevented if we can see them coming. An eternal perspective helps us see life as a journey.

Faith comes from hearing the word. We need to learn what God is like, how to grow in a relationship with Jesus Christ, and to come to believe in God's promises. Charles Spurgeon has said, "The first thing in faith is knowledge. A man cannot believe what He does not know."

We need an identity as a child of God and to feel that we are doing His will. When you fall off the horse, you just get back on and ride. Spending time praying and reading the Bible and other Christian materials help us be more centered. Knowing what we believe is a shield protecting us from the hostility of those whose ideas counter our own and a screen that filters out the junk messages of the information age.

When we get acquainted with God through the scriptures, we can understand the essence of what Paul says in Romans 5:1: "Since we have been made right in God's sight by faith in His promises, we can have real peace with Him because of what Jesus Christ our Lord has done for us."

I know that getting to know God takes time and many middle-aged women think they don't have time to read the Bible, have devotions, and go to God in prayer, but it is the gateway to a better life. Why struggle to get your ducks in a row when God can get them to fly in formations?

Envy

Jealousy comes to the forefront of women's minds more often than we would care to admit. As the old adage reveals, "You can't stop a bird from landing on your head but you can prevent it from making a nest in your hair."

There are things we can do to sidestep these unwanted feelings. Feelings of jealousy and resentment hurt us much more than they do the person who is the target of our envy, and it can retard our spiritual growth. It can be a sign of self-centeredness and immaturity.

Jealousy is not a fruit of the spirit. Although men can become envious of one another's toys and experience professional jealousy, it seems that women wear green-colored glasses more often than men. It speaks of our insecurity.

Many times, women can't get ahead because other women will take them down. There are often treacherous undercurrents of competition in places that employ a lot of women, and family gatherings replete with in-laws also often have their pitfalls. When the fairer sex learns to connect and cooperate instead of competing and comparing, we will all take a giant step forward.

The Bible says that jealousy is a sin. If we are serious about our spiritual life, we ought to be concerned about envy when it happens to us and pray about it.

When we see someone who is doing better than us in an area in which we would like to shine, competition and resentment can raise their ugly heads. It's really hard to take reassurance from the statement "no one can do it all."

Bible study is discovering cliff notes to prevent us from flunking the test known as life. This is not a dress rehearsal. Quit kicking the can down the road, because life is short and we will be held accountable for our actions.

Knowing God's word and accepting His forgiveness can deliver us from misery here on earth and separation from God throughout all eternity. I know that I need forgiveness for the wrongdoings of my past, for my sins of today, and for my sins of every day in my future until I am called home to be with my Savior.

Jealousy is not a justifiable referendum to stab others in the back but rather, it is a signal that we need to develop our character, our talents, and our sense of decency. When we develop ourselves as God wants us to, we will be so busy at improving our own lives that we will forget to compare ourselves to others.

Jealousy and gossip are the sides of the proverbial two-edged sword, and the person most harmed by them is ourselves.

Going Green

All of us have been jealous many times in our lifetimes. When we see others have the material things we would like to have or that seemingly someone "has it made," jealousy is a natural reaction—but it is one that will definitely take us down.

Usually, jealousy arises because we are not satisfied with what we have or who we are. Learn to value your own job, your own husband and children, your own home, your own talents, and your own possessions. Joyce Meyers tells us in her book *Seven Things That Steal Our Joy* that it pays to be happy for others when they are blessed, because if you pass that test, you will find blessings coming into your life as well.

Jealousy isn't a good reason to mistreat someone, but it is a signal that we need to change ourselves or our situation. If we will try to make small improvements daily or weekly, sooner or later, we will find that we are more content with who we are and will be more satisfied with own lives and less envious of the lifestyles of others.

Janine Hall

Envy is a stone around our neck in the sea of life. As long as people are fully engaged in finding someone to hate and be envious of, they may never be able to take full responsibility for their own lives. Instead of wasting time in this manner, we need to take stock of who we are and get busy and try to make the most of our own situation by enlisting God's assistance.

It seems that women wear green-eyed glasses more often than men. It speaks of our insecurity. Many times, we throw each other under the bus because we are jealous. By doing so, we hinder each other's forward progress. When we learn to replace comparing and competing with connecting and cooperating, womankind will take a giant step forward.

It is fruitless to make comparisons with each other, because we are on individual paths on very different spiritual journeys. We are all unique, like snowflakes. Even identical twins have their own special fingerprints.

Competition in areas in which we have no talent is as foolish as a cheetah who despairs that he cannot fly like an eagle and spends his whole life trying to remediate his inability to fly. Always try to be a first-rate version of yourself instead of a second-rate version of someone else.

When we try to damage another's reputation, we are harming at least three people. We are hurting ourselves, the person who is the target of our envy, and the person whom we are enticing to assault another's life and well-being.

Each of us is a masterpiece that bears God's signature. We need to enlist his assistance to help us see and understand why He put us here.

When we discover the purpose He intends for us, we need to fulfill it. We have things to accomplish in the short time we are on the planet. Do everything you do as if you are doing it for the Lord.

The Bible tells us that we should not compare ourselves to each other but instead, we should be about the business of living our own lives. Galatians 6:4–5 reads, "Each one should test his own actions. Then he can take pride in himself without comparing himself to someone else for each one should carry his own load."

We are equal in the eyes of the Lord. We are to treat others as better than ourselves. In the case of envy, "going green" isn't a good idea.

Contains ideas from *Seven Things that Steal Our Joy* by Joyce Meyers

How Much Is Enough?

~~~

Most of us would like to make more money. Many people struggle to make ends meet. But a great number of us want to have more wealth and more possessions to indicate to ourselves and others that we are, indeed, successful.

Many young Americans think that the Great American Dream should happen quickly and in a big way. So they go headlong into a frenzy of getting and spending.

Our society is built on chronic and compulsive consumerism. The mantra of acquisition in our country is to consume, upgrade, and enlarge. We are envious of those who have the status symbols we want, the social position we seek, and the experiences that only money can buy. We suffer from "affluenza."

Albert Einstein said to try to become a person of value rather than a person of success. We need to replace the pursuit of things with the pursuit of character. It is good to have the things that money can buy as long as we don't lose the things that only money can't buy. We need to cultivate a heart of contentment.

We can buy entertainment, but we can't buy joy. We can buy sleep from the drugstore, but we can't buy peace. We can buy acquaintances and companions, but we cannot buy love.

When we count our blessings, we should be thankful. Forgiveness of our sins and the promise of heaven are gifts we don't deserve, but for which we should respond with profound gratitude. Thankfulness is the mother of the other fruits of the spirit and is a people magnet.

Timothy speaks about the rich when he writes "Command them to do good, to be rich in good deeds and to be generous and willing to share. In this way they will be laying up treasures for themselves as a firm foundation for the coming age so that they may take hold of life" (1 Timothy 6:17–19).

Money is a great resource but a terribly inadequate goal. Money has the potential to do great good or the potential to do great harm. Striving for money only is idolatry. The love of money robs us of the simple pleasures of daily living. God very patiently nudges us to pursue righteousness, godly character, faith, love, and endurance instead of being overly concerned with our bottom line.

Covetousness can capsize our lives. The circumstances in the lives of others have nothing to do with your own life experiences. We are all on completely different paths orchestrated by God Himself, so comparisons

Janine Hall

are futile. Anger and jealousy can keep you tethered to despair. I know this is true from personal experience.

Money gives us the potential to make a difference, not just to make a living. Generosity helps others, and it also greatly enhances the quality of the life of the giver. It is a win-win situation. Choose to spend less than you make. Be satisfied with what you have.

> Just think
> You're here not by chance
> But by God's choosing
>
> —Roy Lessin

Identity Theft

We have only to take a long look at the Native Americans to see what happens when a people's identity is lost and they encounter progress that takes them away from their way of life. In order to make it up to them, they all are given money to live on every month. There is more alcoholism, family breakdown, social problems, and despair on an Indian reservation than any place in America.

Liberals want us to join into a world-order government. They want to do that because they see themselves at the top end of the totem pole, and more than anything, they want to rule the world.

They want to downplay people like George Washington, Abraham Lincoln, Dwight Eisenhower, and other icons in American history. They imply that the Declaration of Independence, the Constitution, the Bill of Rights, and other American documents are part of our past and belong in a museum.

Janine Hall

Liberals want us to change with the times, grow, and to evolve into a secular, socialist nation more in step with those in Europe and elsewhere.

As conservatives, we believe there are reasons why the United States of America is exceptional. Those reasons are that we are free to build a life here as we see fit and that capitalism has made us the most successful nation in the history of the planet. We may have problems to address, but we don't want to throw out the baby with the bath water.

If our freedoms continue to deteriorate and the free market becomes the road not taken, don't bother to urge your children and grandchildren to have a lemonade stand or a paper route or to mow lawns. The government will be telling our offspring that there will be three beans in every pot and everyone will get the same amount. Our children may want to know where the beans will come from. Even kids know when things don't add up.

I hope that I've been watching too much Fox TV.

Self-Defeating Ideas

Many of us worry about things that may never happen. It is a useless, repetitive habit.

Mark Twain said, "I've had a lot of troubles in my life most of which never happened." Counting our blessings before we count our cares often neutralizes our anxieties. There is always something to be thankful for.

Matthew 6: 25a reads, "Therefore I will tell you, do not worry about your life—what you will eat or drink; or about your body what you will wear."

We often add to our load by having very high expectations for ourselves. Mistakes feel fatal, and we want to put on perfect performances to ensure acceptance from other people. Conversely, we are disappointed when others fall short of fulfilling our needs and living up to the expectations we have for them.

Everyone has faults, so don't be incredulous when you find them in your friends and family. Sometimes the things people do or say offend us even if they were not intended to be an affront.

We need to accept that the only perfect entity is God. People sin, and they are not here on earth solely to please us. We need to get to the point where we can accept the flawed nature of ourselves and other humans. We can prevent a lot of fretting when we accept the fact that that there are no saints or angels on the planet—ourselves included.

Many people lack the social skills they need to relate well, and some people are just shy. Depression and anxiety are barriers that complicate good communication. Sometimes these tendencies lead to loneliness and isolation. Some people have very few social opportunities.

God did not intend for us to be an island to ourselves. He created in us a need to connect with others. Belonging to the fellowship of believers can fulfill some of our needs for companionship. Joining groups at church and in the community can give us practice at living beyond ourselves.

If our existence is a joyless, godless struggle to survive, we will experience a lot of stress. It is not possible to have a meaningful life experience without a relationship with God. Being indwelt with the Holy Spirit results in a joy that does not depend on life circumstances. God's presence in our lives is the ultimate stress-reduction tool.

Oftentimes, we desperately try to get control over our lives. That always ends in angst because it is impossible to control circumstances in a world where the only constant is change. We need to believe that God is in control and that he loves us and has a plan for our lives. He tells us to "Be still and know that I am God."

If you are lucky enough to feel that you have a well-defined sense of purpose in life, you need to simplify your life and concentrate on your most purposeful areas of endeavor. You need to set priorities and let go of less important commitments.

If you perceive that you have a purpose in life, you are 42 percent less likely to get Alzheimer's or other dementias. If you don't feel that you have a purpose, do some soul-searching and do those things you would do if you thought there was no chance for failure.

A complete acceptance of God's will for your life will result in a huge relief from your load of care. God will live through you and will open doors for you. He will write your story, and the only thing you have to do is hold the pencil and let Him erase the mistakes. Serenity is the gracious gift of peace that we receive for living within the parameters of the will of God.

Relationships

Seek First to Understand

The key to effective personal communication is practicing skills that don't come naturally. We need to learn to listen empathetically in order to get inside another person's frame of reference. Listening empathetically involves a deep shift of intent in our personal relationships. It requires us to take in data that may not be found in our own catalog of information or life experiences in order to grasp what another person is trying to express.

Most of us want to be understood, and we use our "air time" speaking from our own point of view. It is typical for us to listen to others with the intent to reply. We speak, or we are preparing to speak.

If we cannot consider modifying any of our viewpoints after listening to many other people's perspectives, we will go around the same old track until we are in such a rut that extricating ourselves is highly unlikely.

In order to become group-minded and connect with others, we need to get beyond our own autobiography. Asking others the right questions gives them some psychological "air time" so that they can reveal their beliefs, opinions, and life experiences. Because you listen, you become influenceable. Being able to take others' ideas seriously is the key to influencing those around you.

Empathetic listening is risky. It takes security to go deep into someone else's worldview, because you may encounter material much different than what you hold in your own.

In order to put deposits in the emotional banks of the people in your life, you need to validate their experience by reflecting back to them how you think they are looking at their life experiences at that particular time.

The sound of our voice and our body language make up 90 percent of the way we communicate, so we need to listen with our eyes and our hearts. If you can discern the needs of others, you have the opportunity to be helpful to them.

Covey says that "our character is constantly radiating and communicating." Making our thoughts known in order to be understood may not always be met with acceptance. Because we cannot know how others are going to react to our ideas, it is statistically possible that someone will sit in judgment of our revelation of life experiences or personal thoughts. So many times, we are reluctant to reveal ourselves. But if we don't, we can't have the assurance of the validity of our theories, we can't discover common ground with others, or we can't have the joy of saying something that someone really needed to hear.

Reading, writing, listening, and speaking are the four cornerstones of our personal effectiveness. Concerted effort to improve any one of these forms of communication helps us ascend the ladder to a higher level of mental operations.

Knowing the thoughts and feelings of a variety of people helps us to have more rapport with others and have better communication with everyone. It helps to have been around the block.

If you think it's too late to improve your life, it will be a self-fulfilling prophecy and you will be absolutely right. Seeking first to understand others and then trying to make yourself understood will open new vistas, and you will become the recipient of wider horizons and a more accurate outlook on life.

Derived from the book entitled *The Seven Habits of Highly Effective People* by Stephen R. Covey

Rx for Relationships

Connectedness and a sense of community help us overcome our feelings of separateness and isolation. We need to seek relationships with people who encourage us to be all we can be. In his book *Real Magic,* Dr. Wayne Dyer has identified four personal policies that make successful relationships possible.

The first quality that fosters friendships is to relinquish the need to be right. Relationships deteriorate when we need to make the other person wrong or insist on having the last word. Each person has the right to his or her point of view. No one likes to be proven wrong, especially in public.

The second concept for building good relationships is allowing space in togetherness. We all need to allow others to be themselves and to let them have the privacy they need. We need to strike a balance between "we" time and "I" time.

Allowing this kind of downtime is a wonderful gift to our partners and friends. Clinging behaviors or constant togetherness can extinguish the viability of any relationship. Perhaps there is some validity in the old saying "familiarity breeds contempt."

The third important policy that enhances relationships is to limit the idea of ownership. The more we try to limit someone's space by keeping track of them, the more we contribute to the end of the relationship. Ownership is the greatest inhibitor of a sense of purpose and mission in one's life. We do not have the right to tell our partner or friends what they should do in life. No one wants to be dominated or controlled. Our mates and friends actually belong to God—we just get to love them for a while.

According to this author, the last concept that can help us to develop meaningful relationships is an acceptance that we do not have to understand the people we have relationships with. Just knowing that people bring you pleasure is all that is important. We love people because they fill our needs, not because they are just like us.

The author believes that the only barriers that limit the quality of our relationships lie within our own minds. When we are busy improving ourselves any way we can and we adopt policies that facilitate budding relationships, good things are bound to happen.

Put yourself into your relationships. Life is flat without them.

Contain concepts from the book *Real Magic* by Dr. Wayne Dyer

Interdependence

In his book *The Seven Habits of Highly Effective People*, Stephen R. Covey said that we can't have the sweet fruits of relationships if we are not well-rooted in ourselves. He wants to convey that self-mastery and self-discipline are the foundation of good relationships with others.

He conjectures that the self-respect that results from dominion over oneself leads to independence. True independence, at least in the social realm, comes from knowing yourself and being able to control yourself in most situations. Every act of self-control is an act of self-respect. It's difficult to like yourself if you do not know who you are. It's difficult to control yourself if you let other people set the agenda for your personal life or if you let your emotions reign.

Independent thinking frees us from our dependence on our circumstances and other people. It is a worthy goal, but it is not the ultimate goal of effective living. We must learn to think and act interdependently or we cannot reach our full potential.

Independence is all about the *I*. *I* can do it; *I* am responsible; and *I* can choose to act on my environment. Interdependence is all about the *we*. *We* can cooperate; *we* can combine our talents; and *we* can create something together.

We need to take good care of our relationships. The prerequisite of a good relationship is spending unstructured time together. It is a time when independent people become interdependent. The networking that results enriches the lives of everyone involved.

Unless you are a whole, fully functional person, you cannot participate in interdependence. Private victory always precedes public success, so enrich your inner space and then share it with the others around you.

Contains ideas from the book *The Seven Habits of Highly Effective People* by Stephen R. Covey

Synergy

When properly understood, synergy is the highest form of communication and cooperation. Its creativity can bring about new options and alternatives that weren't conceived of by any one participant before those in a group combined ideas and brainstormed.

What is synergy? Simply defined, it is that the whole is more than the sum of the parts. It comes about when people trust one another, respect one another's ideas, and build on each other's strengths.

Good marriages are excellent examples of synergy. This state can bring about fulfillment for each spouse by creating an environment that nurtures the self-esteem and self-worth of each partner.

Synergy is the essence of principle-centered parenting. Covey writes that "synergy catalyzes, unifies, and unleashes the greatest powers within people." In conjunction with the other habits outlined in his book, amazing things can happen.

It takes a large amount of internal security, a sense of adventure, and the power of creativity to become a pathfinder of new possibilities. The essence of these capabilities is just not for entrepreneurs, politicians, and entertainers.

They can happen in the lives of ordinary people with unordinary skills and habits that enrich and transform their quality of life. People with high needs for structure, certainty, and predictability may find creative enterprises to be unnerving or unpleasant. But they shouldn't rule them out as options that may be viable and advantageous later in their lifetime. We all have to start where we are at. The habits outlined in Covey's book are cumulative and are the building blocks of a positive life adjustment over a significant amount of time.

When you go to a wedding and witness the bride and groom light the unity candle, you have witnessed synergy in the making. Teamwork, at its best, fosters unity of purpose and the birth of the creative process.

Persons engaged in synergy communicate and brainstorm until they come up with a solution that is better than any one of them could have come up with on their own. It's better than compromise. Instead of a transaction, it's a transformation. Each partner gets what they want and finds a solution that they're both or all excited about—and relationships are created or enhanced.

Synergy is the crowning achievement of all the previous effective habits and goes beyond independence to interdependence, which unleashes our unlimited human potential. It's a win-win situation.

Derived from *The Seven Habits of Highly Effective People* by Stephen R. Covey

Her Needs

❧

Women have a load of responsibilities in the world of work as well as in the home environment. If they are to succeed at both, they need ample support from their spouses in the marriage relationship. In order to have well-being, they need several crucial attributes in a husband so that they can function at their best. Women need affection and conversation, trust and honesty, financial security, and a husband who is willing to take an active role in bringing up the children.

According to the author William F. Harley Jr., almost all men could use some instruction to get better at demonstrating their affection to their wives. A hug and a kiss in the morning, flowers, a call when he is heading home, or helpfulness around the house send a strong message that he cares about her and wants to show it. Most women like to have conversation about daily events and areas of common interest because it promotes a feeling of unity that leads to intimacy. Willard Harley Jr. recommends spending fifteen hours of quality time together each week when the husband and the wife focus solely on each other.

We need to understand what is going on in our mate's life. We need to inform each other and actively investigate pertinent areas of each other's day-to-day life that is not known to us so we can empathize with our spouses. Women need their husbands to allow a certain amount of venting about negative aspects of their lives without him trying to fix the problem for her. When we can verbalize the things that bother us, they lose some of their power over us. Men tend to want to fix our problems, so they need to be assured that just knowing that they care is often the only remedy we need.

Women need to be able to trust their mates. They deserve accurate information about a man's background and life—past, present, and future. Honesty and predictability are the best marriage-insurance policies.

Women need enough money to live comfortably, and they expect to be supported at a level as well as or better than that at which their father supported them. Couples need to live within their means and reduce standards until they are less stressed financially. If the husband and wife take a common challenge to make ends meet, their spheres of economic expectations are more likely to overlap.

Many mothers would rather stay home, but they feel that they need to work to earn a living or to keep up with the Joneses. Some women want and need a career to feel good about themselves and to feel that they are "pulling their own weight."

Each member of the couple should create a "wants" budget and a "needs" budget and come to an agreement about what they can afford. It is Harley's opinion when it comes to money and marriage that less employment may be more appropriate in order to have a more sane family life.

In addition to providing an adequate income to support the family, wives want and need to have their spouses take an active role in bringing up the children. A father has a profound influence on his children. In addition to giving fifteen hours of undivided attention to his wife, women also want their husbands to have a "hands-on" approach with the children by giving them easy access to their attention and generous amounts of their time.

Harley's opinion is that good parents should take training in order to increase their competency in these all-important roles. The basic tenants suggested by Harley are consistency, learning how to punish properly, and knowing how to reach an agreement with their mates when setting limits and administering discipline. Other desirable parenting skills are learning how to interpret the rules and how to handle anger. The author suggests that parents separate their emotions from their disciplinary actions.

Couples need common interests beyond their parenting roles. Recreation, mutual friends, and home improvements are some of the typical areas couples share.

Hopefully, we as women aren't looking for Mister Perfect, because none of us gals are perfect. Hopefully, women are not hoping to find total fulfillment of all these desirable qualities at the get-go. We all need time to grow and develop.

A family commitment from our husbands gives us the emotional security we need to be good wives and mothers. We appreciate our husbands' efforts and their willingness to meet our needs. They are often nine-tenths of a job well done.

Contains information and ideas from the book *His Needs, Her Needs* by Willard F. Harley Jr.

His Needs

Marriage is a complex, compartmentalized institution. We come to the altar with high expectations of having our deepest needs met and meeting the deep needs of our spouse. The marital golden rule is to meet your spouse's needs as you would want your spouse to meet yours.

We all have a love bank, so it is told. According to Willard F. Harley, in his insightful book *His Needs, Her Needs,* he expounds that our proverbial bank is not designed to be mathematically accurate, but it is simply designed to underscore the fact that we affect each other emotionally. We make positive deposits and negative withdrawals in each other's emotional bank accounts with almost every encounter.

Men and women are made for each other, but our basic needs are different. And many wives don't have a clear understanding of their husbands' love requirements. But we owe it to ourselves and our husbands to be aware of the needs that they feel are important in order to do a better job of covering all the bases.

Harley identifies men's most basic needs to be sexual fulfillment, recreational companionship, an attractive spouse, domestic support, and admiration.

Harley proposes that the typical wife doesn't understand her husband's deep need for sex any more than the typical husband understands his wife's deep need for affection.

Harley maintains that intercourse is the only time a man feels completely accepted, and he only feels sexually satisfied when his wife enjoys the experience of lovemaking as well. The newly married man needs to know that he is wise to teach his bride how to enjoy her own sexuality. If he is affectionate, attentive, and tender, she will respond in like manner to his advances.

Surprisingly enough, men also need to spend recreational time with their wives. Camping, sporting events, going out for dinner, or any happening that gets the couple away from it all ranks second in a man's list of desired facets in a relationship.

Recreation rejuvenates the marriage relationship. Harley recommends finding activities that both spouses enjoy. When you think about it, doesn't this sound like dating? Like the old motto says, "The couple that plays together stays together."

The third wanted trait a man desires in his mate is a good-looking wife. This seems a little shallow, but every wife should attempt to be well groomed, dress nicely, wear makeup, and let her husband know that she does it all for him. Beauty is in the eyes of the beholder, and a good personality is a must, but men want to be seen with a pretty woman.

More well-said: attractiveness is what you do with what you have to work with. If we make an effort to look our best, they are satisfied.

Although most wives work outside the home, it is a basic need for men to have domestic support in that he needs her to be attentive to his needs and to create a positive home environment. When reality sets in, husbands of women who are overwhelmed by responsibility may feel that their needs are the last to be met. It might be advantageous to get some domestic help with some of the household chores if you can afford it. Then wives can be more attentive to their husbands.

Husbands who help their wives on the home front are more likely to enjoy the marriage relationship for logistical reasons as well as because of their wives' appreciation for their cooperation. It seems only logical to me that if husbands want their wives' attention in a very personal way, they should share the home responsibilities in order to make it possible.

Behind every man should be an admiring wife. Harley says that a man thrives on a woman's admiration. It is a big responsibility to create a stable financial environment and to be a dependable husband and father. Our husbands need to be valued and respected by their wives and children.

Filling these needs for our husbands seems to be a tall order. We have the power to build up or deplete our spouse's love bank account. But it won't come to pass by reading about it—we need to deliver the goods and make it happen. But I'm sure that I can speak for all women when I say that to pull it all off, we will need some reciprocity.

Contains ideas from the book *His Needs, Her Needs* by Willard F. Harley Jr.

Men: Who Can Understand Them?

Men and women are not cut from the same cloth. Men take in more calories than we do, dress differently than us, and have different interests than we do. We also need to understand the emotional needs that are peculiar to their gender.

We do not instinctively know how to fill our mate's needs, because they are different than our own. A little time devoted to discerning men's specific needs can reap big dividends in improved marital relationships.

In spite of the evidence to the contrary, what a man really needs is to make us happy. A man's primary goal is to give us fulfillment. If we are unhappy, they feel as if they have failed. Men need acceptance from their wives. They need someone to do it all for.

They need to know that in our eyes, they are a big enough fish to keep. Men want to earn their wives' trust and need to know that their presence in our lives is essential to our well-being.

A man needs the admiration of his wife and family. If he feels that he is your hero, he will outdo himself to continue deserving applause. This is a cradle-to-grave requirement. Your genuine appreciation is the wind beneath his wings. The competition is tough out there, so make him feel that he is special.

Your man needs to feel that although he cannot always please his boss or get along with his coworkers, he is important in the larger scheme of things. Encourage your mate to persist, to make the best of a bad situation, and to keep on keeping on by communicating to him that you appreciate his support financially, psychologically, and spiritually.

Women need to learn the art of empowering their mates. When a woman emotionally supports a man, she can help him to be all he can be. A man feels empowered when he is trusted, appreciated, meets with our approval, and is the object of our respect.

When we try to remake our mates and fashion them into better people, they feel controlled, manipulated, and unloved. Share your feelings without demanding change.

When we learn to support our mate's unique needs, their change and growth will be automatic. When we are putting effort into fulfilling their needs instead of being so focused on our own needs, their love for us will grow and both people in the relationship will become more satisfied. Every man longs to be larger than life.

The Shelter of Each Other

Mary Pipher's book *The Shelter of Each Other* takes a look at family structure and the things in our culture, both past and present, that influence and affect families. Specifically, she addresses the struggles families face in the midst of our current culture.

We are a much more mobile society than we were a century ago. These modern times find us changing schools, taking new jobs, and locating ourselves in communities that are far away from where we originated. This mobility, accompanied by the advent of television, advertising, MTV, computers, and iPods, has changed the values and belief systems of the culture at large. Because our culture is easily accessible and in your face, parents often find their influence to be limited and minimized.

Quality family time is crowded out by a deluge of activities. Often, both parents are actively engaged in the world of work, frantically trying to juggle family and the demands of the workplace. Divorce ends more than 50 percent of all marriage contracts, fracturing the family unit, alienating children from parents, and creating instant poverty. As much as one-third of those below the poverty level are one-parent families.

Through case studies featuring then-and-now comparisons, Pipher continually illustrates the difficulties families face in a culture that often stands in direct opposition to what many would consider safe, sensible, and loving behaviors. Our larger culture has for so long pathologized family love and family membership that it has become the norm for children to disregard their parents, and in some cases, emotionally or physically separate themselves from their nuclear family.

The author discusses lost virtues like character, will, and commitment. Families were once the source of lessons on values and guidance and instructed children how they were to behave. Sadly, for many people, the family has been replaced by a largely media-centered culture that offers up a set of values far different than those most parents would like to convey.

In her book, Dr. Pipher concludes her study by offering up suggestions and examples of family-connecting experiences. She suggests that we develop rituals, histories, and stories that become the ties that bind us together as families. She also recommends that families take the responsibility to reestablish cultural principles that nurture and support children, adults, families, and communities. Her narratives serve as a road map to more peaceful and sane destinations where family togetherness and relationships are enhanced and strengthened.

Contains information from the book *The Shelter of Each Other* by Dr. Mary Pipher

The Battlefield

Divorce is a time of change for the whole family. Relationships are broken or severely strained. Family members don't know how to handle the family breakdown. Many of them feel chaos has set in so they don't know what to do. Both the parents and the affected children experience a lack of stability,

Grandparents can offer a safety net to their adult children and their grandchildren. Your support can make a real difference in the lives of your loved ones affected by this tragic situation.

Approximately half of all marriages end in divorce. Each year, over one million children are affected by their parent's divorce. While most parents realize that their divorce will have an impact on their children few parents know how to be most helpful to the children while adjusting to the dramatic changes divorce can bring.

Grandparents can be a stabilizing force for their adult children and a tower of strength for their grandchildren. A good many baby boomers are raising their grandchildren.

A parent's ability to handle divorce is often an indicator of how well the children will manage. The better the parental adjustment, the better the children will do. Children are most negatively affected by parents who continue to battle after the divorce. Hatred, hostility, and a desire to punish the other spouse compounds the pain of divorce. Research indicates that children suffer the most in bad marriages and in bitter divorces.

Children manage best after divorce when parents keep their differences to themselves and both continue to have an active and positive involvement with the children. Children are not divorcing their parents. A not so good spouse may may be a much loved parent to the child. It is important to remember that most children love both parents and should not be asked to choose between them.

Children realize that that a divorce is a matter of choice. Most often, one of the parents decides to leave the family and no one can make that parent stay. Divorce is an adult decision that has a major influence on the child's life.

Divorce is a tremendous blow to a child's idea that the world is an orderly place. Even though parents have been fighting, children expect their family to last and want parents to work out their difficulties.

When divorce occurs it shakes the very foundation on which the children's life is built. Some children spend a significant amount of time fantasizing that their parents will be reunited and they often need to be reminded that there is nothing they can do to bring their parents back together.

Despite their lack of choice, children are faced with the consequences of divorce. They must adjust to living in two homes and making all the necessary transfers to reside with each parent. In addition, they may move to unfamiliar places and enter new schools. Children may also experience a series of boyfriends or girlfriends or eventually have to accept a stepmother or stepfather.

Divorce often has a negative financial impact on the family's lifestyle. As much as one third of our nation's poverty is created by divorce. It can be a godsend if grandparents can support their grandchildren both financially and emotionally during the onset of the family breakdown.

The grief process for children of divorce is similar to that experienced by a death of a parent. They are mourning the loss of their family as they have known it. They deny that the changes have occurred, are angry with both parents that the divorce has happened, may bargain with each parent about what they will do if their parents would get back together again, experience feelings of depression and loneliness and then finally come to accept their new lifestyle with Mom and Dad individually.

There a number of ways parents can be helpful to their children in the divorce process. Information about the divorce should be spelled out in terms the child can understand. When they understand that blame is not going to be placed on one parent or on themselves children have a better chance to move on and make a more positive life adjustment.

Janine Hall

A counselor, a trusted friend of the family, a grandparent or a mentor can smooth out the bumps on the rocky road of life adjustment for everyone in the aftermath of the breakdown of a marriage.

It should be the goal of every divorced couple to contribute to the welfare of their children by adopting a business like relationship in order to help their children to adjust to such drastic changes.

Grandparent's support and guidance can be immeasurably helpful to everyone involved. Grandparents can help their adult children and their grandchildren weather the storm and to recreate the structure and stability they so desperately need after a divorce occurs.

This essay has been adapted from a paper I wrote in graduate school using information from the Johnson County Mental Health Center in Mission, Kansas

Pain Games

Divorce has shown its ugly face for some of us in the baby boomer generation, but it seems to be rampant in our children's lives. The painful changes and adjustments after divorce affect the whole family. Gaining an understanding of the dynamics of divorce helps us to be effective in helping to heal the hurts of our children and our grandchildren after divorce has occurred.

We can be the pillars of strength that can support the fallen family unit during a chaotic time. Children, by their very nature, crave limits, structure, and stability. You can let them lean on you. Even our married children, who live in a frenzy in these times that assault the family at every turn, need our support and encouragement.

In order to cope with the pain of the breakdown of the nuclear family, the members engage in pain games. See if one or more of these games are being played by your children and grandchildren or someone close to you.

Janine Hall

Don't Worry; It'll Be Okay.

Parents may be in denial that the loss will cause any changes. Instead of admitting that things will be different, parents pretend everything is the same.

The Messenger Game

When angry parents can't or don't want to talk directly to each other, they often opt to send messages through their children. With this option, parents lose control over the content of the message. Children may change a message to fit their needs or deliver a totally different message. This game often gives children tremendous power.

Cutdown

In their anger, parents often say untrue, exaggerated, and negative things about the other parent. Cutdown can be direct when you are saying negative things directly to each other when not in the presence of the children, or it can be indirect when you say the negative things just in earshot of the children. Either way, cutdown hurts the parents and damages the self-esteem of the child and that part of the child that is like one parent or the other.

I Spy

Out of curiosity, parents seek information about their ex-spouse by questioning their children. Getting information can feed anger. Usually, they will tell you more than you want to know, and they do it in such a way that their anger at you is also expressed. This game always puts the child in the middle.

Friendly Divorce

Confusion about your role and uncertainty of how to behave toward each other and toward the children can cause difficulty. Parents may feel that it is helpful to be friendly with each other. If the parent chooses this mode, the children and the parent who was asked for the divorce may be confused about why the divorce occurred. Instead of putting on a friendly front, it is often best to behave in a civil and businesslike manner.

Disneyland Daddy and Merry Mommy

As the parents struggle with how to interact with their children, they feel guilt, insecurity, and loneliness. They try to give gifts and special privileges to make up for the hurt and changes they have caused. What ends up happening is that children have an unrealistic view of family life in which they are always given special treats. The gifts often get larger and more expensive as the child grows. For the child, it sets up unrealistic expectations that life owes them rewards without them really having earned them.

I Wish

This is a children's game of denial that is fed into by the game Friendly Divorce. In "I Wish," children continually hope that their parents will get back together.

When couples are no longer playing these games, it is a sign that they are moving through the grief process.

When divorce fractures your children's home, they and their children are going to need a helping hand from you for a long time to come. Your availability to your children and your grandchildren at these times is important in helping to maintain stability in the family structure, and doing so can give your life meaning and purpose.

Overcoming Ourselves and the World

Christian Purpose— An Overview

Christian Purpose

"Live life with a due sense of responsibility, not as those who do not know the meaning of life but as those who do" (Ephesians 5:15).

Many may not have considered God's word as relevant to their lives because their ways of thinking are secular or they are so busy trying to make ends meet that they feel that they don't have time for godly pursuits. But Jesus Christ is the element that fills the God-shaped vacuum inside our hearts, and it is faith that gives our lives meaning and purpose.

The pentathlon is an Olympic test of endurance and skill. It involves five events, and the idea is for each athlete to do them all equally well. Becoming a Christian gives us five purposes, and it is difficult to do all of them well in order to run the good race. But when we come to faith, we begin to want to please God.

Janine Hall

Fulfilling our God-given purposes has nothing to do with what we do for a living and is not contingent on our social status. Every life can be useful, noble, and God pleasing.

According to Rick Warren, in his book *The Purpose Driven Life*, our five Christian purposes are as follows:

1) "Love God with all your heart." You were planned for God's pleasure, so your purpose is to show love to God through worship.
2) "Love your neighbor as yourself." You were shaped for serving, so your purpose is to show love to others through ministry.
3) "Baptize them into." You were formed for God's family, so your purpose is to identify with His church through fellowship.
4) "Teach them to do all things." You were created to become like Christ, so your purpose is to grow to maturity through discipleship.
5) "Go and make disciples." You were made for a mission, so your purpose is to spread God's message through evangelism.

All the empty promises of the world leave us with a shifting sense of vacancy in our spirits and our souls. We are to turn away from the world and take on an eternal perspective.

Jesus is our rock, the lover of our souls, and the font of reconciliation and grace. Give Him your heart and wake from your slumber of sin, and He will give you purpose, peace, and identity. You will become a child of God.

**Taken from the book, The Purpose Driven Live

Purposeful Living

⚜

We are not accidents. If we want to know our purpose in this life, we need to start with God. He created us and has a plan for our lives. To know Him, we need to study the owner's manual—the Bible—because faith comes from hearing the word. We discover our identity and purpose through a relationship with Jesus Christ.

We were planned for God's pleasure. In Revelation 4:11, Paul speaks about God when he says, "You created everything, and it is for your pleasure that we exist and were created."

We are so important to God that he wants us to live with him eternally. God, the Great Shepherd, takes great pleasure in tending to the needs of his sheep. Ephesians 1:15 says, "Because of His love God has already decided that through Jesus Christ He would make us His children—this was His pleasure and purpose."

God has created in us the ability to enjoy life, not merely to endure it. The reason we are able to enjoy life is because we were created in the image of God.

The peace and love available from a relationship with Christ change life for the better. God loves, delights, and enjoys His creations. Psalm 35:27 speaks of the gifts given to every believer from God's heavenly warehouse of joy and peace when it says, "But it gives great joy to those who come to my defense. Let them continually say 'Great is the Lord, who delights in blessing His servant with peace.'"

Whatever we do to give pleasure to God is a form of worship. The Bible says, "The Lord is pleased only with those who worship Him and trust in His love" (Psalm 147:11).

Anthropologists have noted that all people have a universal urge to worship something greater than themselves. God created us with a built-in need to connect with Him. Worship is multifaceted and takes many forms. Jesus said, "The Father seeks worshipers" (John 4:23).

In his book *The Purpose Driven Life,* Rick Warren states, "Anything you do that brings pleasure to God is an act of worship. Worship should not just be a part of our life, but is should be our whole life." David writes, "Let all who take refuge in you rejoice; let them sing joyful praises forever. Spread your protection over them, that all who love your name may be filled with joy" (Psalm 5:11).

Rick Warren purports that there is a right and wrong way to worship. True worshippers must base their praise only as God reveals Himself to us. Jesus told the Samaritan woman, "True worshipers worship the

Father in spirit and in truth, for they are the kind of worshipers the Father seeks" (John 4:23).

True worship is not a matter of saying the right words. It needs to be genuine and heartfelt. God sees all and knows the condition and intentions of our heart. First Samuel states, "Man looks at the outward appearance, but the Lord looks at the heart."

Worship is not always convenient and comfortable. We may not feel like going to church. We may begrudge the offering we put in the plate. We say we don't have time for devotion and Bible reading. It may be an act of sheer will and sacrifice to worship, pray, give monetary gifts, or to demonstrate our faith in acts of charity and love—but it is required to show God that we love Him and want to please Him and give Him pleasure. A verse to ponder on is: "Love the Lord your God with all your heart and with all your mind and with all your soul and with all your strength" (Mark 12:30).

We were made in God's image to give Him pleasure.

> I asked God for all things that I may enjoy life; He gave me life so that I may enjoy all things.
>
> —Author unknown

*Taken from the book, The Purpose Driven Live

Shaped for Serving God

❧

We are not in this life just to take from it; we were created to give something back. We are called into a life of service. Ephesians 2:10 tells us that "It is God Himself who has made us what we are and has given us new lives from Christ Jesus; and in long ages ago he planned that we should spend these lives in helping others."

We may think that we cannot find a ministry or a purpose, but God created each of us with a special role to play during our lifetimes. What God told Jeremiah is also true for each of us today. He said, "Before I made you in your mother's womb, I chose you. Before you were born, I set you apart for a special work."

Our purpose doesn't have to rival that of Billy Graham or Maw Lucado. God is less interested in what we do than how we do it. He calls us to do common things in an uncommon manner. Great opportunities often disguise themselves in small tasks. Madeline Engle once said, "you are an indispensable part of the great plan. You are needed and you have your own unique share in the freedom of creation."

Albert Einstein once said, "Instead of striving to become a person of success become a person of value." Mature Christians have great value because they are God's diplomats and lead others to the foot of the cross. All of us have a sphere of influence, and God can be seen in us as we meet other people's needs.

Paul reminds us that "God paid a great price for you so use your body to honor God." If we have no desire to make crooked paths straight for those around us, we should examine ourselves to see if Christ is really in our lives.

Once we have found ways to serve God and our fellow man, we are to broaden our experience and deepen and cultivate our gifts and abilities. We can be of service to one person at a time. Paul reminds Timothy to "kindle afresh the gift of God which is in you" (2 Timothy 1:6).

Real servants don't call attention to themselves. They make themselves available to others, pay attention to their needs, and do their best with what they have. Real servants are faithful to their ministry. We are to "put on the apron of humility to serve one another" (1 Peter 5:5).

God is looking for imperfect, weak, and limited people to sign up to do His work. The Bible says, "God purposely chose what the world considers weak in order to shame the powerful" (1 Corinthians 1:27). God enjoys putting His power into very ordinary containers. Paul's second letter to the Corinthians reveals that "We are like clay jars in which this treasure is stored. The real power comes from God and not from us."

Jesus was unmistakable in His admonition to serve God and our fellow man. In Matthew 20:28, He said, "Your attitude must be like my own, for I, the Messiah did not come to be served, but to serve and to give my life."

We are the body of Christ. Many congregations are dying because no one is willing to serve. Mature Christians do not wonder who will fill their needs, but instead what they can do for others out of gratitude for what God has done for them. We need to pray that God will give us the strength to fulfill the purpose that He so carefully designed for us.

Our purpose often can be found in the areas we are passionate about. One rarely succeeds in areas they are not interested in. God molds us through our experience and years of practice of honing the skills we need to serve others.

First Corinthians 12:6 reads, "God works through different men in different ways but it is the same God who achieves His purposes through them all." We are shaped by our families, our education, our vocation, our social experiences, and our faith. God allowed these unique happenings in our lives to mold us into the person He intended us to be in order to fulfill His purposes here on earth.

We have within us the pieces of others' puzzles, and we need to give those pieces to them. Conversely, other people have information that we can benefit from, and we need to know what it is. God designed us to need each other and to be interdependent as we strive for brotherly love.

God allows us to go through painful experiences in order to prepare us for a ministry to others. Who better to mentor a new widow than one who has walked in her shoes? Who better to understand the sting of poverty than one who endured it themselves? The Bible says, "He comforts us in all our troubles so that we can comfort others. When others are troubled, we will be able to give them the same comfort God has given us" (2 Corinthians 1:4). But in order for us to use our painful experiences, we must be willing to share them. When we do so, it is a healing experience for all concerned.

The good news of the Lord is incredibly important and eternally essential for all of us. Consider the fact that we have such a short time to share it. Prayerfully search for a significant ministry of your own.

**Taken from the book, The Purpose Driven Live

Formed for God's Family

❦

"God is the one who made all things and all things were made for His glory. He wants to have many children share His glory" (Hebrews 2:10).

Throughout the Bible, we see the evidence that God wants to bring as many people as He can to love Him and call Him Father. His chosen people were destined to be a part of God's family; He is the vine, and we are the branches. The Bible says, "His unchanging plan has always been to adopt us into His own family by bringing us to Himself through Jesus Christ. And this gives Him great pleasure" (Ephesians 1:5).

The family of God consists of all the believers in the past, all the believers in the present time, and all the believers that will come to faith in the future. When we accepted Jesus Christ as our Savior, God became our father and we became His children. Jesus said, "My mother, my sisters, and my brothers are all those who hear God's word and obey it." Luke 8:21 tells us that "In a miraculous way He is capable of providing

It's My Turn

all those who believe with their most intimate and absolutely essential relationship that spans eternity."

The body of believers gives us solidarity, a oneness in purpose and a source of fellowship. Our relationship with other believers inspires us and supports us to keep us in the one true faith. Galatians 3:26 tells us, "You are all children of God through Christ Jesus."

We are all created by God, but not everyone is a child of God. To become His child, we must have a spiritual birth. When we deny our old sinful self and all its capacity for wrongdoing, we die with Christ. Then our spiritual self is born, and we experience a newness of life. We become more and more like Him.

The Bible says, "When I think of the wisdom and scope of His plan I fall down on my knees and pray to The Father of all the great family of God—some of them already in heaven and some down here on earth" (Ephesians 3: 14–15G). Our relationships on earth are important and necessary. The love between a man and a woman is a beautiful and hopefully lasting thing. A family reunion is a joyful occasion and a chance to reconnect with our roots, but it is nothing compared to the perfect love relationships we will have with our Maker and all the saints in heaven.

Our eternal inheritance is unmatched here on earth, and it is permanent. There is no power on the earth or in hell that can take away our home in heaven or separate us from Christ. The Bible reassures us that "God has reserved a priceless inheritance for his children. It is kept for you pure and undefiled, beyond the reach of change and decay" (1 Peter 1: 4).

Contains material from *The Purpose Driven Life* by Rick Warren

We Were Created to Become Like Christ

~~~

"Let your roots grow down into Christ and draw up nourishment from Him. So that you go on growing in the Lord and become strong and vigorous in the truth" (Colossians 2:7).

In the book *The Purpose Driven Life,* Rick Warren reveals that it was God's plan to create us to become like Christ. God announced that intention when He said, "Let us make human beings in our image and likeness" (Genesis 1:26).

We were created with four characteristics that make us like God. Like God, we are spiritual beings who are immortal. Our spirit will live eternally, unlike our body, which is mortal and temporary. Because we have a soul, we are able to experience God's presence. We are capable of having a relationship with God, who is the everlasting, all-knowing center of the universe.

The Bible says that Jesus was "the visible image of the invisible God" (Colossians 1:15). God wants His children to bear His image and likeness. Because man had free will and chose to sin, man became incomplete, and our image was distorted.

Because we were not able to reinstate and reconcile our ability to be like Christ on our own, God the Father sent Jesus to earth on a mission to rescue us and restore a right relationship with our Creator that we were not able to accomplish without His help.

God endowed us to be intellectual beings. He designed us to be able to think, to reason, and to have the ability to solve problems. We should be thankful for these attributes and put them to good use to intentionally imitate our Savior and fulfill God's purposes here on earth.

The Bible points out God's intention for the way we should live when it says, "Take on an entirely new way of life—a God fashioned life, a life renewed from the inside and working itself into your conduct as God accurately reproduces His character in you" (Ephesians 4:22–24).

God wants us to live in the center of his will, but we continually try to control the circumstances of our lives as if we know better than God what should happen to us. Some people go so far as to postulate that we can become a god. The New Age philosophers have the misguided, arrogant, and narcissistic mind-set that we all are gods capable of being holy.

Like God, we are relational; that is, we are able to give and receive love. God is the source of love. The good news that God loves us in spite of our unlovely state of being is mentioned very often in the Bible, but

Janine Hall

nowhere as succinctly as John 3:16, which reads, "For God so loved the world that He gave His one and only Son so that everyone who believes in Him will not perish but have eternal life."

When we are able to realize how much God loves us and accept Christ as our Savior, we become a member of the body of Christ and will want to pass this love onto those that are around us. The Bible tells us, "Each part gets its meaning and function as a part of His body" (Romans 12:4–5).

We are capable of taking on the character of Christ. God is far more interested in molding our character and purifying our faith than caring about our position in society, our accumulation of wealth, or what we do for a living. He wants us to have the faith of a child.

Jesus did not come in order to provide an easy and comfortable life for us. He does not promise us a rose garden. He uses our experiences, both good and bad, to make us more like Him. Second Corinthians intimates that "As the Spirit of the Lord works within us, we become more and more like Him and reflect His glory even more."

We are to turn away from the world and develop an eternal point of view. We are to be in the world but not of the world. The Bible warns us, "Don't become so well adjusted to your culture that you fit into it without even thinking. Instead, fix your attention on God. God will bring out the best in you" (Romans 12: 2).

Pay attention to the things God's trying to teach us in His word and through our life experiences.

**Taken from the book, The Purpose Driven Live*

Mission Possible

❦

"Be ready at all times to answer anyone who asks you to explain the hope you have in you, but do it with gentleness and respect" (1 Peter 15b–16).

Becoming a Christian gives us the opportunity and the responsibility to influence the people in our lives. God is at work in the world, and He wants us to join Him in the mission to spread the gospel. Jesus said, "As the Father has sent me, so I am sending you."

At age twelve, Jesus told His parents, "I must be about my Father's business." Twenty-one years later, He died a cruel death nailed to a cross. His last words were, "It is finished." Rick Warren stated that "Like bookends, these statements framed a well-lived, purpose driven life." Christ completed his mission that the Father sent Him to do.

If you found the cure for cancer, wouldn't you want to share that cure with everyone that has that dreaded disease? We all have a sickness called sin that leads to spiritual death. If we have the "good news" of salvation, shouldn't we tell it to those we love, as well as well as to those we don't know? The saved will enjoy the forever favorable conditions of heaven. We should be sharing the message now before it's too late.

Joining God in His mission in this world gives our lives meaning and purpose. William James said, "The best use of life is to spend it for something that outlasts it." The kingdom of God is the only thing around that has eternal implications.

Most people are going down the wide road that leads to destruction. We have the responsibility to share the Gospel, and you and I are the only ones who can reach a certain set of people. We have a motivation problem. Paul said, "My life is worth nothing unless I use it for doing the work assigned to me by the Lord Jesus—the work of telling others the good news about God's wonderful kindness and love."

The consequence of our personal mission is that winning souls is more important than our careers, our worldly goods, and our secular prestige and power. Many of us have tunnel vision that rivets our attention on the here and now.

Most of us, if not all of us, are interested in our own welfare. In Philippians 2:4, God commanded: "Don't think only about your own affairs but be interested in others too." We need to make the difficult mental paradigm shift from our self-centered thinking to other-centered thinking. Becoming "born again" gives the grateful convert the desire to pass it on.

The apostle Paul said to his prayer partners, "You are also going help us when you pray for us." There is real power in prayer. Intercessory prayer is the most effective tool we have we have to help others. As Rick Warren said, "People may refuse our love or reject our message but they are defenseless against our prayers."

The world situation is the catalyst that may help us change our thinking from the here and now to an eternal perspective. When we turn away from the world, it helps us to determine what issues are the most important in life. Paul said, "So we don't look at the troubles we can see now, rather, we fix our gaze on the things that cannot be seen. For the things we see now will soon be gone, but the things we cannot see will last forever" (2 Corinthians 5:4).

Wouldn't it make your never-ending day to see someone you care about in heaven because you helped them see the light? What are you waiting for?

**Taken from the book, *The Purpose Driven Live*

Green and Growing:
Personal Development

Identity

There are many factors that form our personal identities. Instead of feeling integrated and whole many of us don't have the slightest notion who we are. If that is true for us we need to do some soul searching and introspection in order to meet ourselves and get acquainted. We need to do some excavating into the strata under the surface of the face we show the world. Self-discovery is the first step toward self-appreciation.

Thousands and thousands of learning events, verbal and non-verbal, behavioral and emotional have shaped us into who we are. We are sculpted by our environment and our life experiences.

Our growing up nuclear family is the greatest earthly influence on our identity. Early childhood experiences mold us because our personality is formed by the age of five or six. Our birth order is a significant factor. Grandparents can also enrich our childhood and give us additional role models. They can help point us in the way we should go. Other extended family can also be influential if we are fortunate enough to live near them and see them often enough to know them well.

Some of our beliefs and ideas come from the people in the locality where we are born and raised. Moving to different places during our lifetime exposes us to new ideas and different ways of doing things and can broaden our horizons

Part of our identity comes from our own generation and its influence on our thinking. Time changes things. The world you grew up in was a different place than it was at the time your parents came of age. Your children had to cope with things that never existed when you grew up. Only a contemporary can truly understand the forces that formed any particular generational mindset.

If you would find yourself you need to think for yourself. If you rely on others to make your decisions, you will never know if your own ideas are valid. The advice of others can be invaluable in times of trouble, but for the most part we need to learn to chart our own course.

When we have a relationship with Jesus Christ the major part of our identity is derived from being a child of God. His love gives us joy that becomes our strength. Our purpose is to be intimate with HGod and to love and serve others.

When you realize that God created you and loves you just the way you are it is easier to love and accept yourself. He has a purpose for your life. No matter what our occupation is it is only a part of who we are. Coco Chanel has stated "How many cares one loses when one decides to be someone instead of something." It is especially important to discover yourself before the end of your career in order to make a smooth entry into retirement. Then you can plan purposeful activities you will enjoy when you no longer leave the house to go to work in the mornings.

What parts of you are beneficial and attractive to others? What parts of you are counterproductive and need changing? What parts of you were there from the beginning? What parts of you are hidden underneath the surface and need to be expressed in some way?

Who you are is singular and unrepeatable. You are God's masterpiece. Learn to accept who you are and let God work through you.

Self-Acceptance

When we look at our mixed bag of abilities and disabilities, personality traits, likes and dislikes, birth order, and other characteristics, we often look around and think we would love to have the traits we see in someone else. In many ways, our talents and intelligence are decided at birth by our Creator. Sometimes, we don't know how we can make a contribution, and we don't see the relevance of Socrates's assertion to "know thyself." But self-awareness is the first step toward self-acceptance.

In a sense, we all have to play the hand we're dealt. Robert Louis Stevenson said, "To be what you are and become what you are capable of becoming, is the only object of life." Dare to be yourself without apology.

Think about the kinds of relationships you had when you were growing up. These relationships are the gateway to similar social alliances in adulthood.

Think about the things that you were good at or enjoyed in an earlier stage of life. These characteristics might have the potential to be hobbies much later in life and may develop into meaningful pastimes in retirement.

To illustrate how one can do these things, I will use my own life as an example. I am aware of how my past relates to my present and my future.

I was five years old when my brother was born. I also was the first grandchild on both sides of the family for several years. My birth order category is the one of the "super firstborn," because my personality was formed before I had to share the center stage. My peers were my grandparents, my aunts and uncles, and other adults. To this day, I am most comfortable with people older than myself and have a good number of close relationships with senior citizens.

It has been pointed out to me that I've reached that category myself. I share some of my philosophy of life with this group honoring the time-worn ideals of God, country, and family.

I also connect with people a lot younger than myself. I think that it true because my second brother was only three when I left home and because it is a common trait of firstborns. That is probably why I became a teacher. My brother was a second grader when I began my teaching career in a second grade classroom, and that helped me to know what to expect.

I am unable to tolerate all the strains and stresses of traditional employment at this time. I am also a bit of a free spirit and I like to be my own boss, so I am self-employed. I have worked selling home décor to other women for thirty years. It is a passion of mine to beautify my home, and it is an avenue of self-expression.

I am also an author, and my writing occupies a considerable amount of my time. Creativity has made a profound difference in my life in the last seven years. When I'm writing, I am in a world all my own.

School was always important part of my life, and I still think of myself as a student. I have three degrees, but more importantly, I am a student of life.

Firstborns tend to be competitive with peers their own age and have fewer successful relationships with them. This is the personality trait that is hardest for me to accept. I have a few friends my own age, but I'm not comfortable with the women of my generation until I know them well. I have abandoned my old modes of competition and comparison and instead have been trying to connect and cooperate. I've read that this switch is a part of entering the fifties and sixties. All my relationships have improved since I have adopted this attitude and I have learned to network.

I am less of a perfectionist, and I am learning to dismiss the qualities that fall short in myself and others. No one can be all things to all people, and we all wear a tag that says, "as-is" or "slightly irregular." We are all works in progress. It's fascinating to see other people grow, and it's a source of sincere gratitude to experience it in myself.

Because I had problems with depression at different times in my life, I was not very motivated. The traditional female role was not a good fit for me by any stretch of the imagination. It was like the chicken and the egg. I don't know if I was depressed because I was inactive or inactive because I was depressed.

God has delivered me from that muck and mire and I'm never going back there again. God is slowly transforming my life as only He can do. Old parts of me are awakening and flourishing. The latest positive quality reappearing in myself is the capability for me to be at one with nature.

There was a time when I was stigmatized by my shortcomings. I felt inferior because I didn't like to cook or sew, and I had some issues that separated me from other females. I was too dependent on my spouse.

On the inside, all I need for identity is to be a child of God. The parts of me that others can see are my greeting-card ministry, my love of decorating, and my writing. I was the chairman of the McCook chapter of Christian Women's Club for two years and have completed nearly forty Bible studies in the period of the last seven years. I was a substitute teacher for many years.

Grandparenting is a new role for me and is now my connection with children. I have a circle of friends who protect me from those who would be my detractors. My husband was my greatest earthly source of contentment. He passed away two years ago, and I am learning to spread my own wings. I have everything I need. I am thankful for God's grace and loving kindness *and* I like who I am—a servant of Jesus Christ.

Green and Growing

We all are not what we once were. Thousands of life events—verbal and nonverbal, behavioral and emotional—have shaped our psyche. Any number of sculptors have shaped our clay. It truly does take a village of role models to launch a successful life. The things we did not get from our parents can be obtained from other significant persons in our life journeys.

Growth requires change and effort. Helen Keller said, "Character cannot be developed in ease and quiet. Only through experiences of trial and suffering can the soul be strengthened, vision cleared, ambition inspired and success achieved."

When integrity is compromised, self-esteem is the first casualty. We all know when we have disappointed ourselves. Dishonesty is a stumbling block, and it corrupts our character a little at a time. Honesty is displayed in actions and not words. An honest appraisal of oneself is the beginning of wholeness.

Many of us lack the intestinal fortitude to be ourselves. Some of us can be our real selves with some people and not with others. Perhaps we have chosen colorlessness as a camouflage and do not want to be different so we will not be judged. Frustration and self-pity arise from not being ourselves.

Experts say that in order to break an addiction or any other means of avoiding life, we must deal with the feelings that are being masked. Trying to escape pain by running from it creates more pain. To take steps toward wholeness, we have to be willing to feel our own pain. Allowing ourselves to experience our legitimate suffering is the pathway to higher ground.

This is inconvenient and is difficult to do because we all have things we need to do—such as working our jobs, living with our families in our domestic realms, and dealing with our relationships with our friends and coworkers. Yet if we do not persist, we are on a treadmill to nowhere.

Forgiveness is the atomic power of personal growth. Release bitterness, hatred, and resentment. Feel them as they leave your mind and body. Establish a quiet time, and let the reservoirs of your soul replenish themselves. Find the source of your feelings and the place deep inside you where the still, small voice of God speaks to you. It can tell you many things. Before a doctor can prescribe a remedy, he must first diagnose the disease.

Similarly, then, we cannot correct our character flaws until we unearth them. Until we realize that a certain behavior pattern is self-defeating, we cannot eliminate it. When we stop doing it, it will die of attrition. Then we will be freer to evolve into happier and healthier people.

Forgive yourself for dreaming larger than you live. To dream and fall short is so much better than not to dream. Realizing that we may not reach all our dreams is the beginning of maturity. We are just human, after all. Look around and you will see many others that have come to the same conclusion.

Positions of greater responsibility are often difficult and not to be envied. Being ordinary is not to be nondescript because of the fact that we all are so different from each other. Each life has a purpose, but it sometimes takes a lifetime to solve the identity enigma. Learn to lean on God.

> When one door of happiness closes, another opens; but often we look so long at the closed door that we do not see the one which has opened for us.
>
> —Helen Keller

Confidence

Sometimes, women feel that they need permission to be goal-oriented because they think all their efforts should be focused on supporting others around them. Nevertheless, achievement is the sail of self-esteem, so we, too, need little victories.

The best and most satisfying source of confidence is from God. When we submit to Him, He will lift us up. It is from confidence in His promises that we draw our strength. The largest portion of our identity consists of being a child of God. When He takes up residence in our hearts, we will begin to make good use of the talents and interests He gave to us.

Joyce Meyers, in her book *The Confident Woman*, explains it this way: "I am confident in my leader God, and the gifts, talents and knowledge He has placed in me. I know that without Him I am nothing but He brings out the best in me."

Janine Hall

God won't allow any meaningful experiences in our lives until we submit to Him and become dependent on His grace. His grace allows us to be the unique person He designed us to be. We then have permission to be ourselves and we can quit pretending to be something we are not—what a relief!

I used to try to be like my husband because he seemed successful and highly regarded. I desperately tried to emulate his strong points in areas in which I had no natural ability. We are about as opposite as two people can be. Of course my performance was second rate, and I felt that I had failed. That's why it is so important to develop our own talents or pursue the things we have an interest in. That is our destiny. When we let God unfold our purpose in life, we become more vibrant and viable persons.

Without the confidence that God instills in believers, even simple accomplishments elude us and are beyond our grasp. Fearful women cannot reach their full potential. They become people pleasers, and therefore, they can be manipulated by others. Fear cripples performance.

Joyce Meyers suggests that "Fear is like a an emotional virus because it begins as fearful thoughts in your head. Then it affects your emotions and behavior."

With courage and God's help, one can walk through open doors into the unknown. If we live in the cave of our own self-recriminations, we will never feel the proverbial sunshine on our faces.

We can be highly educated and financially successful, but until we submit to God and have confidence that He will bless us, we are like a brand-new car with an empty gas tank. We won't get anywhere. God gives us power for living as a means to chart our journey on earth and to our final destination in heaven.

But we must be persistent in our efforts. Max Lucado had his first book rejected by fourteen publishers before he found someone who would give him a chance. NBA superstar Michael Jordan was cut from his high school basketball team. Henry Ford went broke five times before he succeeded.

Many of us think ourselves into disaster. Pessimists look at the land of milk and honey and see calories and cholesterol. We feel a little bad and we fill our minds with the thought that we are sick. We start out the day with the dread that something bad is going to happen.

We look to tomorrow with fear and trembling. The trouble we fear becomes a self-fulfilling prophecy. We need to quit predicting disaster and say with the psalmist: "This is the day the Lord has made. Let us rejoice and be glad in it." A confident person recovers from setbacks.

When our bodies become a temple of the Holy Spirit, His joy will become our strength and confidence. God promises to make life full of good things for those who believe in His promises and are obedient to his will. He does not change, and we can have confidence in His assurances and in His protection.

David wrote that when "The righteous cry, and the Lord hears and delivers them out of all their troubles." James 5:16 reads, "The earnest prayer of the righteous person has great power and produces wonderful results."

Janine Hall

We need to ask God to prevent us from wanting the things of this world more than we want the safety and security of a holy life.

Ninety percent of what we worry about never happens. Some things seem bad at the time, but later you can see that they were necessary for our growth and development. Joyce Meyers reminds us that God disciplines those that He loves.

Many successful persons all through history have taken God's promises seriously. Try it—you'll like it. We have his ironclad guarantee. Therein lies our confidence.

Contains thoughts from *The Confident Woman* by Joyce Meyers

Contentment

Our society is built on chronic and compulsive consumerism. Advertisements on the radio, television, and in magazines and suggestions from others in our environment convince us that we need to acquire, consume, upgrade, and enlarge. We are seduced into thinking that our personal value is measured by our bottom line.

Money is a great resource but a very shallow goal. An obsession to acquire wealth is a self-feeding fire. The "love of money" is an aspiration that can overtake the rich and the poor alike. First Timothy 6:10 admonishes us to examine our motivations about making money when he said, "Some people eager for money have wondered from the faith and have pierced themselves with many griefs."

It is good to have the things money can buy, provided we don't lose the things that money can't buy, such as integrity, character, love, faith, and contentment. When we put God and other people before possessions in our hearts, we are sowing seeds of enduring satisfaction.

Janine Hall

The things of the world have no lasting value. Life in this world is like the game of Monopoly. No matter how much or how little you acquire at the end of the game, it all goes back in the box. God alone is the source of life.

Contentment is a decision to be happy with what you already have. We must desire God's blessings more than we desire wealth to have our priorities in the proper order in the biblical sense.

Spouses cannot give us a sense of our own worth or value. Only God can give us love, peace, and true belongingness. Deep-seated satisfaction is a gift from God resulting from faith in Jesus Christ. The disciple Paul's words are striking: "Godliness with contentment is great gain."

When we realize that God loves us, we can rest in the knowledge that everything works together for good for those who love the Lord. We all can find completeness serving others in the particular way He has called us to do.

Instead of making the acquisition of wealth our most important goal, we should choose generosity as a lifestyle, no matter how inexpensive those gifts may be. We can also give others our time, our attention, and our love. If our motivation is genuine love, compassion, and a willingness to help, we will stumble onto the amazing discovery of "God's mathematics."

If we are persons who give to others, God will reimburse us in many ways. We will find that no one can out-give God. God's blessings naturally follow the generosity of those who show obedience to God's command to give to others in a plethora of different ways.

We need the peace that passes all understanding to help us deal with the economic woes and social unrest around the globe. Then we can say with the psalmist, "I am content and at peace. As a child lies quietly in its mother's arms so my heart is quiet within me" (Psalm 131:2). Christ calls us to be *in* the world but not *of* the world.

Contains material from *Seven Things That Steal Our Joy* by Joyce Meyers

No Jesus. No peace. Know Jesus. Know peace.

Creativity

❧

Jeanette Moniger has postulated, "Tapping into your creative side can combat stress, boost brain power and make you happier." Studies show that optimal health is not just all about good eating habits and proper exercise but that using our creative side also has a profound effect on our well-being.

I've been interested in beautiful things since childhood and have been working for a decorating company for decades. Since I've also begun to write creatively, my ability to accessorize has improved well beyond the staid and static results of my efforts in years gone by. I've also been able to arrive at more original ways to solve problems that would not have occurred to me in the past.

Although I had done regular and crewel embroidery, I shied away from most "craft projects" because I felt I had no talent and I thought I would fail. Early in my creative writing days, I thought I would also try to arrange flowers and was pleased with the results. I was surprised and decided that in former days, I had just believed I couldn't do arrangements and was therefore bumping my head on the glass ceiling of my own low opinion of my ability to do those kinds of projects.

For a while, I was into making my own greeting cards. The results were by no means professional, but I enjoyed doing them and people seemed to enjoy getting them. It was good therapy. When I was restless, bored, or had the "blahs," creating something that I could see gave me a feeling of accomplishment and enhanced my self-esteem.

Shelley Carson, PhD, author of *Your Creative Brain: Seven Steps to Maximize Imagination, Productivity and Innovation in Your Life,* said that "you probably perform hundreds of creative acts every day." Creativity consists of finding original solutions to problems and new ways of looking at old situations. Rearranging your furniture and accessories, solving a business dilemma, or finding new ways to stretch your family budget engages our creative thought process.

Using your creativity has a myriad of benefits including stress reduction, improved brain function, and enhanced mood. According to research done at the Massachusetts General Hospital's Institute for Mind Body Medicine, the author reported that "the repetitive action of creative tasks like knitting or crocheting create a relaxation response and can lower blood pressure." Our grandmothers could have told us that many years ago. Creative pastimes are good therapy.

You can engage your creative side by reorganizing a closet, improvising on an old recipe, or taking new routes to familiar destinations. Douglas Pagels has said, "Expressing your creativity is done more by the way you are living than by any other gesture."

Janine Hall

According to an anonymous source, "Adaptability is the power to make a suitable environment for oneself out of any set of circumstances." It takes creativity and flexibility to land on your feet when new life situations present themselves in a world where the only constant is change.

According to Moniger, there are many studies that show that creative activities are an excellent mental defense against age-related memory loss. People who regularly stimulate their minds by doing home repairs, playing an instrument, painting on canvas, making a quilt, or any other creative pastime are three times less likely to develop Alzheimer's. Creative ventures produce confidence and mental clarity.

Creative activities release serotonin, a feel-good chemical that can play a significant role in fighting depression and anxiety. A survey of knitters and crocheters found that 42 percent of respondents turned to their craft when they wanted to combat stress. Some say the feeling of accomplishment in the midst of a creative venture can result in a state of mind not unlike a runner's high.

As we age, we often become set in our ways and suffer from tunnel vision. Creativity is one way we can get outside the box and still engage in play. We don't stop playing when we grow old—we grow old when we stop playing. A 2007 *Journal of Health and Social Behavior* study revealed that creative people feel as much as seven years younger than their actual age.

Many women like to have something tangible to show for their time because much of the results of their work are invisible. I feel a connection with other creative women and am experiencing a greater acceptance of the female role because I have created things. The following source speaks about how we can live creatively when it discloses that "Every artist dips his brush into his soul, and paints his own nature into his pictures."

Exercise, creativity, spirituality, and a good diet are part and parcel of the fountain of youth. Women's strengths of intuition, creativity, and mystery give us special ways to serve each other and give us trophies to lay at Jesus's feet.

Contains information from the book *The Art of Living Well* by Jeanette Moninger and *Your Creative Brain: Seven Steps to Maximize Imagination, Productivity and Innovation in Your Life* by Shelley Carson, PhD

Lights, Camera, Action

※

In his hierarchy of needs, Abraham Maslow suggests that anyone can live creatively. People in all walks of life can create artistically, find new ways to reinvent themselves, find new relationships, and find new ways to make contributions to the welfare of others. We are the directors, producers, and the leading ladies of our own particular life dramas.

Conditions that are conducive to living creatively are a high level of knowledge and/or experience, freedom from criticism, internal motivation, and the power to control one's own ideas and work. It's never too late to begin.

Living creatively often involves simplicity. Following every whim leads to confusion. Specialization brings about clarity and conciseness.

Often, on television programs, a current event creates the need for an expert. Usually, someone comes forward and shares his or her knowledge about a subject and in many cases has written a book that sheds light

It's My Turn

on the matter at hand. This common occurrence illustrates the benefit of specialization.

Of course, as everyday women, we rarely have the in-depth knowledge in an area of expertise, and neither would we want to. But on a smaller scale, personal identity and confidence can come from being knowledgeable and creative in the areas of cooking, crafts, gardening, music, decorating, recreational reading, writing, and many other areas of personal expression. Our careers can help us to grow and develop as individuals. Our spiritual lives add richness and meaning to our everyday existence.

In the larger scheme of things, independence, freedom, and the ability to control our own destiny are the main components of the Great American Dream.

In a smaller scale, using our talents and developing our interests engenders a sense of usefulness and productivity. One does not strive for perfection, because in doing so, we would negate the purpose of creating in the first place.

Social skills, the ability to empower others, and the desire to be helpful can sculpt careers and modes of living. Relationships are created when we are open with others and spend unstructured time with them. A new alliance can open a whole new vista of life experience. Barbara Bush once commented, "Cherish your human connections; your relationships with friends and family."

Many people feel, and rightly so, that they don't have the luxury of time to stay connected with others. Brief phone calls and greetings at

Janine Hall

Christmastime can be used as steppingstones in time to help keep our relational channels open.

It is important to adjust to a changing family structure. Children leaving the nest and marrying necessitates letting go of close family ties. Our maturing children often need financial assistance. Caring for aging parents is both a privilege and a cause for concern and calls for frequent monitoring and close attention. The birth of grandchildren is a welcome event, but it also is an adjustment for everyone concerned.

Finding more creative ways to live calls for some out-of-the-box thinking and consideration of the viewpoints of others. We all have a boredom threshold. Going around and around in the same old track creates a sizeable rut—a rut that kills spontaneity, creativity, and the zest for living.

God is the most creative entity in the universe and has formed everything that exists. Ask for his assistance in finding some viable new ways to negotiate life.

Have confidence in His promises. Be open to new experiences.

Uncovering a Multitude of Sins

Women have a hard time dealing with conflict, even within ourselves, and it's hard to recognize our own false pride. We are expected to be peacemakers, and we feel uncomfortable voicing our resentments even to God, so we stuff them inside and go on.

Some women are hardened by the stresses of the workplace and the problems of life and run over other women who get in their way. We get our feelings hurt, nurse our wounds, and quit speaking to each other, sometimes never to be friendly again.

In the give-and-take in the work to be done on the job or on a volunteer basis, people inadvertently bump into our old wounds and sensitive areas. We are not always good at identifying the issues we need to work on or fully understand them.

Sometimes God will send us a friend or a mentor to talk to who will help us fit the pieces of our puzzles together into a meaningful whole. Often, we need to deal prayerfully with one issue at a time. Sometimes, it is just high time for spring-cleaning, and the garbage we've been carrying around needs to go.

Maybe we don't want God or others to know our thoughts, but we're not fooling God, because He knows all. And sometimes we are also not fooling other people. When we share our past deeds or a present situation with our pastor, a counselor, or a trusted friend, we open up the portals of our heart. The pent-up shame and guilt, the hurt and humiliation, and the festering anger emerges.

Some radio and television ministries have prayer partners that are ready to pray with you. Admission of our wrongdoings is the first step. We may think that past deeds or decisions were wrong but that they don't affect us now. We want to leave sleeping dogs lie. But Christ wants to reclaim all of us and set us free.

Often, there is little others can do but hear us out and pray for us. But God can untangle our messes and clean up the consequences of our sin. We need to open up the crusty compartments and dank corners of our hearts. Then the sweet-smelling fragrance of redemption can begin to fill every corridor of past experience.

We may have to remove a few layers of false pride to discover the real beauty of a clean heart and a right spirit. Penitence is the prerequisite of peace.

We need to humble ourselves before God and admit that we cannot thrive without His help. We must vow to seek His guidance and be obedient to His directives.

George McDonald once said, "How often we look upon God as our last and most feeble resource. We go to Him because we have no other place to go. And then we learn that the storms of life have driven us not upon the rocks, but into the desired heavens."

Little by little, Christ's living waters permeate over our past like much-needed moisture into the parched earth after a long drought. In his letter to the Romans, Paul asks of his readers, "Don't you realize that you have become a slave to sin, which leads to death, or you can choose to obey God which leads to righteous living. Thank God! Once you were slaves to sin, but now you wholeheartedly obey this teaching we have given you. Now you are free from your slavery to sin and you have become slaves to righteous living."

After the enormous blessing of forgiveness for our sickness called sin, the fruits of the spirit well up inside us, and our relationships come to life.

It's a process, and it can be a long one. Why not get started today?

Personal Management

~~~

Personal management is all about the breaking down, the analysis, and the specific application of the important tasks in one's life. It's the ability to make decisions and to make progress. It's central for the housewife, the businessman, the college student, or the city manager.

The fourth habit of highly effective people is to have an independent will to improve one's lot in life. Author Stephen Covey states that "Empowerment comes from learning how to use our greatest endowments in the decisions we make each day."

We need the drive to complete the important activities to reach our goals that are born from our core values and the talents God gave us.

Everyone has so-called "urgent" things to do. These things consist of activities like getting to a doctor's appointment, cooking the evening meal, continuing education, meeting deadlines, going to work, or paying taxes. Urgent things are visible and require our immediate attention.

But so often, we are so busy doing "urgent" things that optional, more important tasks are neglected.

The trouble with urgent tasks is that we get to thinking more and more things are urgent. Our perfectionist tendencies speak to us and say we must have a spotless house, a nice yard, a good job, and community involvement.

Some endeavors that are more important than urgent things and that are not visible to others are the prevention of future problems, relationship building, planning our lives, recreation and exercise, and—most especially—a relationship with God.

Covey says to ask yourself which one of these traits keeps you from getting the important things in your life accomplished: 1) the inability to prioritize, 2) the inability or desire to organize around those priorities, or 3) the lack of discipline to execute and stick with the projects that are important for you to accomplish. Furthermore, Peter Druckers suggests that we feed our opportunities and starve more unproductive activities by conscious design.

People who have priorities that are important to them may resist becoming efficient because it would lead to a lack of spontaneity, rigidity, and an "all work and no play" existence. Covey said to *be* efficient with things but *have* effectiveness with people.

Because your relationships should be highly valued, you should be ready to change your priorities or postpone tasks in order to honor and cultivate them.

Janine Hall

While we walk the tightrope of doing the day-to-day activities of living and managing the home, we may be stealing time from the things that give us companionship, purpose, and identity. Invite a friend for coffee instead of completing the laundry in record time. Work on your quilt instead of polishing your kitchen. Do your genealogy research instead of attending a meeting you "should" go to but have little interest in. When all is said and done, how will you be remembered? Will it be at the expense of really living?

Integrity is our ability to make and keep commitments to ourselves and our ability to walk the talk. You have to think about what you would really like to do in life, take steps to carry it out, enlist the help of others, and find satisfying roles to play.

Making a quilt, writing a book, landscaping your yard, or improving your job performance takes discipline and the ability to delay gratification. Choose what you would like to accomplish in your life and then be true to yourself.

Contains ideas found in the book *The Seven Habits of Highly Effective People* by Stephen R. Covey

> Things which matter most must never be at the mercy of those things that matter least.
>
> —Goethe
>
> To affect the quality of the day—that is the highest of the arts.
>
> —Henry David Thoreau

Let God Be God

We are not smart enough to run our own lives. God's ways are higher than our ways. When we struggle to control our destiny and to create a blueprint for success, we experience frustration and turmoil.

We need to retire as God's assistant. Instead of trying to *make* it happen, we need to *let* it happen. When we let God orchestrate our puppet show, we bypass excessive worry, over-analysis, and our thinking that we need to pull all the right strings.

The Bible says that our lives won't have meaning and significance until we have a relationship with God. If we think we know everything, there is no need to trust God. Trusting God means living with unanswered questions, being patient to wait on God, and believing that He has our best interests in mind.

Janine Hall

If you do what you usually do, you will get what you usually get. Relying on the Holy Spirit will often lead us away from the worn-out recordings of our favorite songs.

We need to be subject to change when we get the inner knowing that we should consider new options when they present themselves.

If we don't have some kind of plan, we will never accomplish anything. Enlisting God's help is the smartest thing we can ever do. Proverbs 16:9 reads, "A man's mind plans his way, but the Lord directs his steps and makes them sure." Let the Holy Spirit brood over the waters of your life, and let Him lead you into green pastures.

Life is not meant to be so complicated. We need to quit trying to understand everything. It is amazing how quickly God can make crooked paths straight. Proverbs 3:7 exhorts us to "Be not wise in your own lives but reverently fear and worship the Lord."

It isn't an oversimplification that life is a big "yes and no" question. We want to say yes to God and accept His willingness to guide and help us instead of trying to treat life as a do-it-yourself project. Turn things over to God and do your best to live a God-pleasing life. Take this divine advice: "Be still and know that I am God." (And you are not!)

Risk

An anonymous source once challenged the reader to "Go out on a limb because that's where the fruit is." If you want to make your life more interesting, satisfying, and dynamic, it will involve change, and change doesn't happen without risk. There is truth in the old saying "Nothing ventured; nothing gained."

Changing your ways is not easy. It is very hard to break old habits or to form new ones. It is a matter of retraining the brain. That takes time and a great amount of effort, but it is within the realm of possibility. It's never too late to become what you might have been. Take your example from the turtle that doesn't get anywhere unless he sticks out his neck.

A new situation is often unsettling, but with persistence, it becomes less scary. If you've ever had to relocate to a different area and cultivate new friendships, you can appreciate how difficult it is to readjust and go forward. Because many of us have attempted this daunting task by necessity, perhaps we have gotten better at taking calculated risks. All human relationships involve risk.

Janine Hall

There is no self-esteem in passivity, inactivity, and outdated modes of living that don't work for us anymore. Most people fear the unknown, but when we get right down to it, it's not the actual event that we dread but the fearful feelings and the unpleasant sensations that will accompany a new assertion. When we learn to walk through the open doorways to new experiences, we will say to ourselves, "That was very scary, but I did it anyway and with repetitions, it will eventually get easier. Good for me."

If we find ourselves in a relatively isolated position in life for any reason, it is hard for us to evaluate our own experiences because we have nothing to compare it with. Rating our own reality will become more accurate when we have frequent socialization. Just being with people and listening will be of help. When we observe what others are thinking and experiencing, we can get more grounded in what is going on around us.

A life without relationships is a lonely and fearful existence, and our personal locus of safety cannot be enlarged without risk. As it is with many things, a new enterprise or endeavor can begin with the smallest of steps. Enlarging our social circle or attempting new things can be made possible by taking several little risks every day or week. After several months, evaluate your progress and see if you have captured a happier, more robust lifestyle. Be satisfied with small gains because from small beginnings can come great things. Participation is important.

Our self-esteem is enhanced by recognition from others, but it is largely defined by how we see ourselves. If we do our best instead of barely getting by, if we do the right thing even when no one is watching, and if we find ways to serve others, our estimation of ourselves will rise. Others will respond to our newfound self-respect with interest.

Nothing worthwhile is gained without risk. We must not, in trying to think how we can make a big difference, overlook the small daily differences we can make, which over time add up to be big differences that we often cannot see. Frequent little moves outside our comfort zone can snowball over time and can help us achieve a more meaningful and purposeful life experience.

It is a risk to marry, a risk to have children, and a risk to take a job or train for a career. Even making the Christian leap of faith is a bit uncertain because we cannot see down the road. Not taking risks is the biggest risk of all. Little acts of courage are the building blocks of life.

Courage

> It is not because things are difficult that we do not dare; it is because we do not dare that they are difficult.
>
> —Senaca

> Courage is found in the first forward stride,
> Standing your ground, not stepping aside.
> Sharpen your focus and let your eyes see,
> Not where you've been, but where you can be.
>
> —Jan Weimers-Woolwine

> You cannot launch if you don't leave the beach.
>
> —Anonymous

Simplicity

◈

Eleanor Roosevelt said, "a little simplification is the first step toward rational living." When we take stock of our lives, many of us need to react with gratitude.

When we realize how much we have, we should feel the urge to pare down, get back to the basics, and learn what's really important. Perhaps good by-products of the recession are realizing the difference between a want and a need and deciding to examine our priorities.

Year by year, the complexities of this spinning world grow more bewildering. So it becomes more and more important to seek peace and comfort in joyful simplicities. Once you've found the things you most like to do, specialize and focus on them. Decide to do a few things well, and let the rest of the world go by like a long parade.

Give yourself permission to choose your options, to pick your battles, and to find time for yourself. First Timothy 6:6 intimates that "A devout life doesn't bring wealth but the rich simplicity of being yourself before God."

There needs to be more sanity in life—a reduction in activities. Corrie ten Boom advises us to "avoid the barrenness of a busy life." The way to do this is to concentrate slowly on completing one task at a time while eliminating all areas of endeavor except the ones that give us identity and purpose. We are not called to live up to the responsibilities of others but to our own.

It is not selfish to do the things we enjoy. We need quiet joy as much as we need food and shelter. Think of it as therapy that will make you more pleasurable to be around.

Having quiet time and enjoyable pastimes mellows out our attitudes and gives us something to share with others, especially with those who share our passions. A quilting club is a good example of a group that has a common interest and provides the participant with social opportunities as well.

Give yourself little vacations from the rat race. Things won't seem so overwhelming when you return to duty. When we dash here and there and take on more than we can handle, life becomes like a three-ring circus with no pause between acts. We have no time to let the reservoirs of our souls replenish, no time for reflection, and no time to make conscious contact with our Maker.

Always being busy can keep us from living our lives by crowding out reality and avoiding our issues. Constant activity robs us of the unstructured time necessary for us to develop relationships. Friendships die of attrition when we fill our calendar with commitments every moment of the day or are on the Internet for hours on end. The ability to make conversation may be a casualty of the information age.

We need to spend time with our families and friends. These opportunities for fellowship may never come our way again. No amount of worldly success can compensate for failure at home and the loss of the quiet joy of companionship. Having a few good friends and a circle of acquaintances provides us with shelter from the storms of life.

Women are pressed from every side to conform to the standards of this world and to rearrange our biblical priorities. We need to depend on the Solid Rock for support when we find ourselves in a whirlwind. No one can make us take on extra responsibilities without our permission. The psalmist says to "Find rest, O my soul, in God alone; my hope comes from Him" (Psalm 62:5).

There is more purpose in quiet reflection and prayer than in a wild rush of getting and spending. Deliberately turn away from the world, and listen to your authentic self and the whispers of God. Learn what you can live without.

Restore a sense of rhythm to your life. Children aren't the only ones who need regular mealtimes, regular bedtimes, and time for solitude. It isn't only in decorating that less is more. Simplicity is the common thread that stitches us together. Take joy in the commonplace.

Solitude

In the book *Simple Abundance*, Sarah Ban Breathnach tells the reader that "Too many of us approach time alone as if it were a frivolous expendable luxury rather than a creative necessity." Just under the surface, there's a place of restful reverie where we can experience rejuvenation and where we can sense God's presence.

Certain springs are tapped only while we are alone. The artist must be alone to create, the writer to express his/her thoughts, the musician to compose, and the saint to pray. Women need solitude in order to find the essence of themselves.

Regular periods of quiet time are essential for emotional and spiritual growth. When you can go without "noise," you are learning to be at peace with yourself, and you have grown. Achievements in our outer environment must have been first conceived and believed by our inner selves. That can only happen in solitude.

Janine Hall

Solitude is voluntarily and temporarily withdrawing to privacy for spiritual purposes. R. J. Foster has written, "The less we are mesmerized by human voices the more we are able to hear the Divine Voice."

Deliberately turn away from the world. Wean yourself away from the opinions of others as you continue the journey within. Attend Bible studies and church, because hearing the word is a prerequisite of faith.

We are not socialized to appreciate solitude. We think that if we are not constantly engaged in busyness that we are not pulling our own weight. Productivity is not only action oriented. Creativity rich in alternative solutions for living does not thrive in the maddening crowd. The Holy Spirit is stifled by a whirlwind of activities.

Preparedness that comes from forethought, rest and recuperation from the care of the day, and communion with God are essentials that result in better life adjustment.

Solitude replenishes the reservoirs of our tranquility. Anne Morrow Lindbergh suggests that "If women were convinced that a day or an hour to themselves was a reasonable ambition they would find a way of attaining it. As it is, they rarely make the attempt."

Solitude helps us to avoid burnout. We need to retreat to be like Mary for a time in a decidedly Martha world. Silence the overzealous inner slave driver that pushes you to do it all. There is merit in the maxim that tomorrow is another day.

Solitude cracks open the door that separates the outer world and the inner self. Spend some time with God, who created you and has a plan for your life. We need to tie up our loose ends before our joy in life completely unravels.

One author suggested penciling in a half an hour before and after work to collect your thoughts and read the Bible. Take a half an hour and soak in the privacy of the bathtub. Claim two hours of your own on a Sunday afternoon. Use it for your renewal.

Taking time for yourself is an act of self-love. You know when you've had enough and need to retreat. The fresh perspective that you will gain will be helpful in dealing with the rest of the day.

Some people have more privacy needs than others. Some firstborns or only children will need more quiet time because they often were alone when their personality was formed. People who grew up in a large family can tolerate longer times of togetherness because they grew up in a crowd.

Most retired couples would tell you that when you retire, you shouldn't try to attempt a marriage marathon of being together every waking moment of the day. Most retired people need some space of their own. You will soon learn to accommodate your mate with time for themselves and time for outside socialization. One source suggested that you should think twice before you retire to a small apartment because it is difficult to maintain your personal boundaries when it is hard to get away from each other.

After our children are launched out into the world, we have an increased opportunity to spend time with God and to do the things that were an impossibility when our offspring lived under our roof. We can say, "It's my turn," and use our time to develop our God-given potential.

Steps toward Serenity

Begin with the End in Mind

~~~

Another integral habit that is the hallmark of highly effective people is personal leadership. When we have an accurate assessment of what we will need to do to accomplish a goal, we need to develop a game plan. A necessary component of every successful goal-setting is to begin the plans with the desired end in mind.

When a woman plans a dinner party, she thinks ahead and decides how to best serve her guests and how to see to it that they enjoy themselves. She chooses a menu that she knows will turn out well, plans to decorate her table, and chooses what dishes and napkins to use. She responds warmly to her guests to help them feel at ease and may plan to play cards or have other forms of entertainment. Before she begins to make preparations, she has the desired end results in mind and can visualize everyone enjoying him- or herself.

If you have a baseball and a baseball bat but success in life is contingent on tackling the opponent, catching passes, and running to the end zone, obviously, your performance will be poor. If you are driving through Denver with a map of Los Angeles, you haven't a prayer of finding your destination. You need to have a basic understanding of what it takes to be effective in reaching your goals. If you don't have a set of successful strategies for a positive outcome in any area of your life you can learn them and acquire new, more effective life skills.

We need to lean on God, but at the same time, we need a certain amount of self-leadership. Inefficient self-management in the ocean of life will be, as one individual phrased it, "like straightening the deck chairs on the Titanic instead of steering away from the dangers below."

In order to know if you're charting the right course, you need to visualize the final outcome—beginning with the end in mind. A win-win strategy must first come from within. Anything that happens in your outer environment must have its origin in inner realization and requires planning.

If you don't like yourself, know yourself, or have confidence in yourself, other people will accept your own low opinion of you. Be thankful that a relationship with Jesus Christ can transform you and make you feel significant. We do not have confidence in ourselves but in what God can do through us. Without Him, we are nothing, but with Him, we cannot fail because "With God all things are possible" (Matthew 19:26). He has your best interests in mind.

The modern-day Christian is a like a small boat in a torrent of unrelated, confusing, and disconnected ideas. But we can reach our destination by the way we set our sails and by keeping our eyes on Jesus Christ.

It's My Turn

Once we find a Christian purpose in life, we can count on the robe of righteousness to cover us, protect us, and give us security. We will no longer be a puppet on the strings of popular opinion. Instead, we can live in the center of God's will. God is the solid rock.

If we try to make our lives God-pleasing, we will be blessed by God. God will pick us up when we fall, welcome us back when we stray, and forgive us when we sin. No one can walk the perfect walk. That's why Christ did it for us. In this way, He was both the perfect sacrifice and the perfect example of a sinless life. We can become more like Him in our faith journey by being dependent on the Holy Spirit.

If we focus on timeless, unchanging truths from the Bible, our personal ability to act wisely will increase dramatically. The Bible is not just an old, outdated book filled with myths written by uneducated men a long time ago.

It is the living, breathing truth inspired by the Holy Spirit that can help us in our day-to-day living. Study it to get the "big picture" of salvation, redemption, and eternal life.

Then the rest of your life can begin, with the end in mind, and you can press on to win the prize.

Contains some ideas from the book *The Seven Habits of Highly Effective People* by Stephen R. Covey and some Christian truths from the Bible

Differentiation

The more well adjusted persons in any family are those who have achieved a separate identity. Any member who is overly dependent on the family unit feels a lack of self-sufficiency and that causes angst for the whole family. Dependency cripples the self esteem of the member who is unable to stand alone.

Overly timid or overprotected children and overly dependent wives may not perceive themselves as having individuality. Overprotected or sheltered family members are like the dogs who never leave the porch. They do not know what is going on in life because they get their information second hand. Knowing what you believe cannot be inherited or borrowed. Each person must determine their own world view and unfold their own identity in order to develop and mature.

The main thrust of maturation is to have individuality and separateness. People cannot develop their own personhood if they don't know who they are.

Janine Hall

There is a difference between being a helpmate to your husband and being enmeshed. No one wants to be joined at the hips with their mate playing hopscotch throughout life. Codependency is not a good goal.

In order to find yourself you need to think for yourself. That doesn't mean that you should counter every idea your husband has and become defiant and combative. It just means that you should have an opinion.

In her book The Confident Woman, Joyce Meyers says we should liken our marriage to a road trip. Both partners need to determine where they want to go in life, look for landmarks, and find the right paths in life in an equal manner. But the man is the one who turns on the blinkers and actually turns the car. (Of course stopping to ask for directions is a whole different subject—right???}

If you or someone else in your family isn't thinking for themselves and is too dependent enlist the help of family and friends to help them come out of themselves and find out what it is to feel the sunshine on their face. God is the only entity we should be dependent on after the onset of adulthood.

Individuality and differentiation from the family mass is not easily attained but no one else can do it for you. It takes a great deal of courage to strike out on your own if you've been dependent on others in your family for a long time but the benefits of personhood cannot be overstated. The longest journey begins with a single step.

Myopia

Many times, we do not see life as it is, but as we are. A writer once said, "The same blossoming cherry tree looks like a profit to the grower, a painting to the artist, a bookcase to the woodworker, and a feast to the birds." The lens through which we see the world is colored by our own perceptions. We project what we believe onto the world around us.

If we feel lesser, then we will interpret events in such a way as to reinforce our feelings of inferiority. If we feel superior to others, we will believe that the actions of others often confirm our own high opinion of ourselves.

If we are depressed, the "gray-colored glasses" of our own pitiable condition will color our whole perspective. The world will seem like a dreary, dreary place, and we may feel helpless and hopeless. We then need intervention to see life not as we see it but as it is and how it can be.

To clearly envision a better world and a better us, we will have to be willing to understand that some our beliefs—especially those about ourselves—are mistaken and that we must throw away our old, gray-colored glasses. We feel badly because of the debilitating and erroneous opinions we have about ourselves or others. These lies are only beliefs, and beliefs can be changed. We must remove the log in our eye in order to see life without distortion.

We need to be willing to be persuaded that our viewpoints are not accurate and to make an attempt to develop a different, more positive perspective about ourselves and others. Many people are victims of cruel situations, but with God, all things are possible, and He can restore us to wholeness a little bit at a time.

Reading, or bibliotherapy, as it is called, broadens our horizons and helps us to better understand life and ourselves in order to have a better attitude about life.

Individual or group counseling may be advisable. The best kind of counsel can be with our friends and family. A relationship with God can transform our whole being and bring healing to our minds and hearts.

New inner experiences can create new outer realities. When we begin to see ourselves and those around us as works in progress, there is ample room for hopefulness, because no one is a finished product and we will continue to grow until we go to be with the Lord.

When we begin to think that the world is a friendlier place, it is probably due to changes within us. God can awaken us from unpleasant scenarios into brighter scenes as we begin our transformation. Growth often means change and a letting go of old, tired scripts and creating new, brighter, and happier realities.

Yes, this a sinful, fallen world, but we can transcend the world because Christ first did it for us. There are other mature Christians that can mentor us in a walk with the Savior and help engender the world of change that only He can provide.

We are in the world but not of the world. Separate yourself from the world, and join the church that is waiting for the bridegroom to reappear. Deny the sins of self-gratification and make a conscious effort to become more like Christ.

When we open our spiritual eyes just a little bit and see God, we will realize that much of our vision problems were due to the darkness of the world. The prescription for our ocular problems is Jesus Christ. When we walk in the light, we experience joy that does not depend on outer circumstances. We will realize that we are a part of a network much larger than ourselves, and we will then experience true belongingness.

He is the vine, and we are the branches.

When we focus on the eternal, we experience a paradigm shift as we realize that life on earth is short and our next address will be heaven. We need to spend time with God every day so we can see where we are going and not lose heart for the journey ahead.

> When you pray go into your room, close the door and pray to your Father, who sees what is done in secret, will reward you.
>
> —Matthew 6:6

Janine Hall

Faith is a grand cathedral, with divinely pictured windows. Standing without, you see no glory, nor imagine any. But standing within, every ray of light reveals a harmony of unspeakable splendors.

—Nathaniel Hawthorne

Discomfort Dodging

Real satisfaction comes from a lot of effort and the desire to achieve goals. Comfort-seeking, on the other hand, involves the avoidance of effort and difficult but fruitful tasks. When things get stressful, we don't like the glib comment, "It's tough all over."

Consider the comfort level we take for granted in modern life. We want someone to mow our lawn and shovel our snow. We hire someone to clean our homes, we eat fast food, and we want constant entertainment. We are addicted to the "fun factor," thinking if it isn't fun, why do it?

Those who are characterized by discomfort dodging drift through their days and weeks with little direction. I know of what I speak, because in former days, I had a PhD in comfort-seeking and avoiding tasks that I thought I couldn't do or were too hard for me to accomplish. We think that things are beyond our skill level or we just don't want to do them, so we take the easy way out.

Consider the athlete who practices his sport repeatedly every day. Think about the employee who has worked in the same place for many years. We would like to have the prestige or the security they enjoy, but we are unwilling to duplicate the effort required to master a task or don't want to make the investment of our time to refine a skill.

For several reasons, I am best at something I can do independently, so I have been self-employed for several years. If you truly can't succeed in traditional employment, you need to seek out alternative ways to make money and make contributions to society.

Some Americans indulge in the instant gratification of too much food, so we have an epidemic of obesity in our country. We can't make ourselves give up momentary pleasures in order to gain long-term benefits. We are a nation of discomfort dodgers. We are too soft on ourselves in many ways.

Needless psychological misery mounts up from an unwillingness to accept the frustrations of everyday life. The procrastination of difficult or unpleasant tasks is destroying the integrity of our workforce, our moral fiber, and our ability to work toward long-term goals. When you couple discomfort dodging and a sense of entitlement, the result is widespread dysfunction.

There are ways to gain skills that will help us to learn to delay self-gratification. In his book *Do It Now,* Dr. William J. Knaus listed ways to increase the ability to delay gratification and learn to wait patiently. He lists a number of examples that could be helpful. Perhaps you'll want to adopt some of the following suggestions.

- When feasible, have dessert fifteen minutes after completing your meal.
- Systematically put a predetermined amount of money into a savings account each payday.
- Start a hobby like needlepoint that requires time and concentration to complete.
- Be early to appointments and meetings with friends. Bring a book along to read if you have to wait.
- Order something from a catalog so you will have to wait to see if you like the item when you get it in the mail.

If you don't want to deal with the displeasure and inconvenience of a great amount of effort in any capacity, you will probably have a fruitless life.

Many people can bear much more mental discomfort than they think they can, or they don't realize that hard work is the precursor of self-respect. Those with mental and physical handicaps need our compassion and assistance. But everyone needs to fully engage in some kind of fruitful endeavor so they can experience self-worth.

Abraham L. Low, a modern-day psychiatrist from the 1950s, identified us as living in a "culture of comfort." It's not fun to diet, to do well in school, or to maintain a strong work ethic with persistent effort. If you do what you usually do, you will get what you usually get, so muster up some willingness to dive in with both feet.

We know what we want concerning material things, but we don't want to bear the discomfort of waiting until we can save the money for them.

Janine Hall

We think that frugality stinks, and we don't want to be thrifty or cut out unnecessary purchases.

Go the extra mile. Take rest breaks, but give it your best effort. Be intentional in all areas of life. Work at your relationships, your job, and maintaining your home. God expects us to be good stewards of ourselves, our talents, our property, and our time.

Punctuate your life with needed downtime, but put your shoulder to the wheel and give it all you've got. Work is not fun, but it creates dignity and self-reliance.

Comfort-seeking behaviors are tough habits to break. Most of us really dislike being uncomfortable. But in order to be successful (whatever that means to you), you need to experience new little victories for a renewed sense of self-esteem.

Don't be discouraged because of a strenuous race. There will always be some high hurdles on the way to the finish line, but with God, all things are possible.

Feel Your Feelings

It seems that in our American social milieu, we divert our attention to something else if we see that someone is obviously struggling emotionally. We all want to create the illusion that everything in our lives is going well and that we are on the top of things. But when we deny our emotions and conflicts by pushing them down under the level of our awareness, we are only fooling ourselves.

When someone is coming over to see us and we don't have much time to prepare, we may toss all the things that are cluttering our house into a closet and shut the door. When we toss all our unresolved mental messes into the back recesses of our mind, they can create anxiety and depression, and it may become necessary to deal with them one by one in order for us to feel like ourselves again.

Women are socialized to be peacemakers, and we are very uncomfortable with conflict. We strive to avoid our negative emotions by hoping they will dissipate. It is hard for us to break "the niceness barrier" and express our true emotions when they are negative.

Our repressed emotions can bring us down like a rock thrown in a pond. We might have layers of resentment, anger, and unresolved conflict underneath the surface.

God can help us deal with them by forgiveness, repentance, and cleansing.

Instead of avoiding our unpleasant emotions, we need to unearth them, own them, and feel them. When we encounter these troubling feelings, we need to experience them in all their misery in order for them to evaporate and be gone from our lives. Fears that we will be stuck in our problems' negativity are unfounded, because feelings will rise and fall if you let them.

Just as we go through stages of grief when losing a loved one, dealing with other negative emotions also has stages that we need to experience. In order to overcome our depression, anger, and fear, we need to walk down the valley of our own negativity in order to be free from them. But the good news is that we never have to walk the walk alone, because God is right there with us. God knows what is on your heart, and He is everywhere at once, so take His hand. Together, you can face all things.

We all need to face the reality that once we have worked through a problem, another one will inevitably present itself front and center. But as we continue this process, we will become stronger and more able to respond to the challenges and storms of life. The perceived degree of difficulty of our problems will seem to go down because we will become stronger and more resilient.

Just as in the grieving process, the last stage we have to go through before resolving our conflicts is despondency. This is the stage we all would like to avoid if at all possible. But if we will embrace the negativity, we will inevitably emerge out of the depths with a restored sense of well-being and renewed energy. It is a birthing process—joy is borne of pain, and we go on to higher ground.

Walk through your valleys knowing that you will never walk alone because God is by your side. Be comforted in the knowledge that you will rebound from your difficulties with God's help. This, too, will pass. The wider and deeper the valley, the more joy, peace, and strength will be yours when you traverse it.

Your Coming-Out Party

꧁꧂

Because of the frantic pace of modern life, many women don't have the time or the opportunity to make other women friends and maintain those relationships. Stay-at-home moms sometimes suffer a sense of isolation from a lack of adult conversation. Working moms are so busy working and raising a family that they lack time for themselves, let alone time for other significant relationships.

E-mails and the Internet are a poor substitute for face-to-face social experiences. Clubs dissolve, people die, situations change, and neighbors move away. Frequent relocation is not an "environmentally friendly" circumstance for making friends and finding new companions. In some communities, "transplants" are still seen as outsiders, even after many years. Developmental stages such as the empty nest or retirement finds us at loose ends looking for new social opportunities.

For one reason or another, we may find that we have become relatively isolated. Maybe your best friend moved away. Maybe you have outlived your siblings. Perhaps you are recently divorced or your significant other is in the military on the other side of the globe. After a long time in a situation like this, you can forget how to make a friend or form relationships with certain segments of the population—or perhaps with anyone.

Sometimes we are closed off because we don't want to get hurt again in some way. Perhaps we are afraid of opening up to others, so we are building walls instead of bridges. It's just much easier to stay at home rather than to venture out and take social risks.

Starting over again just seems too formidable a task, so we ignore the problem and wait for others to make the first step. It's not as hard as it seems. The perceived degree of difficulty of making relationships will decrease as your level of effort and self-respect increase.

I experience fear and anxiety every time I meet a new person or begin a new money-making venture, a new Bible study, or any other social opportunity. But I've learned the difference between living *in* fear and living *through* fear.

I have learned to step out toward freedom while I pass through the dark recesses of a frightening new situation. I always take the Great Shepherd with me and He helps me find my way.

Maybe you need come out of yourself into new arenas. Coming out is not for sissies and the faint at heart. It takes courage, persistence, prayer, and a willingness to experience a lot of stranger anxiety.

It is uncomfortable to come out of hiding. If we are not connected with anyone else, we experience the feeling of not knowing what is going on in society. Then we begin to worry about whether our version of normalcy matches up with the versions the others in our environment who seem to know what is going on.

Over time, we can learn to tolerate the presence of others and learn to experience intimacy again. Keep in mind that we are all more alike than different and that the Bible tells us that we are not experiencing anything that is not commonly known to man. Those around you may be experiencing similar problems.

If you have some shameful secrets (so you think), they need to be told; you are probably overestimating their importance, and you may be working possibilities into probabilities about their consequences. Many of us have wild imaginations or perceive ourselves as the center of the universe.

Think of your reentry into social discourse as earning a degree in reality. Become involved in a few social situations. Take in information from each of them and try to look for commonalities and reoccurring patterns.

Instead of making judgments, just gather data. Each experience will provide you with another piece of your puzzle. Possible scenarios can include: going to church and Bible studies, making friends with a neighbor, having coffee with a group that is already meeting, taking up quilting, joining a card group, or going to see a counselor. Visit shut-ins, or engage in any activity that may come your way.

Each experience can be another brick in the foundation of your new, revised worldview. God is the only mandatory component in all our lives. You can learn something valuable from each experience. Try to see things from the perspectives of others, and get outside your comfort zone to meet and greet those who are in your environment. I feel that I can learn something from everyone I meet. It is things you learn after you think you know it all that are the most helpful.

Looking for a quick fix is setting you up for too-high expectations and disappointments. It only takes one night to see the stars, but it can take a lifetime to reach them.

Accept that you may need to change the beliefs you have about yourself and others because the symptoms you are experiencing may be the direct results of how you perceive life.

When you have had a lot of different life experiences, you will find your reality base and you will form your philosophy of life. Be patient in your spiritual life. God promises that those who seek Him will find Him.

PS—Go out and buy yourself a new outfit. It's your party.

Decisions, Decisions

Men have traditionally made most of the larger decisions in married life. Many women know their own minds and are adept at making choices. But for various reasons, some women make so few choices that their decision-making process is weakened from disuse and they cannot make up their mind about anything without difficulty.

If you find yourself in this category, you are not alone. You need to flex your decision-making muscles in order gain more independence, more ego strength, and a greater sense of self.

Start out with small decisions that have little or no consequence. Get out your clothing and create some different combinations that you haven't worn before. Decide to go for a walk several times a week. Get out that old set of dishes you haven't used for a long time and invite someone for coffee.

Make a prioritized list of tasks each day and cross out each task as you complete it. Decide to take a new route on your way home from work. Clean out your drawers and cabinets so you feel more efficient. In order to minimize stress, tell yourself that you will do a task at a specific time in the near future that you can't get done when you planned to. And then follow through.

Every time you make a small decision, you will become more and more able to make larger decisions. If you don't go to church, attend one next Sunday and consider making it a habit. Consider joining some kind of social club in order to meet new people. Choose to confront someone you have a conflict with.

As your ability to make good choices increases, you will be more able to successfully engineer the direction and quality of your life. Big decisions that greatly affect your life should be made carefully, thoughtfully, and prayerfully, such as what career steps you want to pursue, whom you will marry, and where you shall live. If big decisions have very negative results, we need to decide they are not written in stone.

Make life choices to help those around you, and then don't talk about it. These choices build up treasures in heaven and self-respect here on earth.

Spouses can give us human love, but it is Christ that provides us our most basic love and belongingness needs. Receiving God's infinite love and forgiveness and responding to Him with love and gratitude opens the love channel in life. Then God asks us to love others the best we can because He first loved us. Help and be kind to others without expecting anything in return. God will see that these deeds will not go unanswered. His blessings will beat a path to your door.

Our earthly possessions and prestige are desirable, but only the decision to accept the love God has for us is deeply satisfying and supplies all our needs. David puts it this way in Psalm 103:5: "He fills my life with good things. My youth is renewed like eagles." When we experience intimacy with God, we can say, "This is the day the Lord has made. Let us rejoice and be glad in it" (Psalm 118:2–3).

We all have the choice of going down the wide, alluring, attractive, and well-traveled road of earthly pursuits. Or we can go down the narrow, more difficult road that is only chosen by a few. The Bible records Jesus's words about the road to heaven in Matthew 7: 13–14: "You can enter God's kingdom only through the narrow gate. The highway to hell is broad and its gate is wide for there are many that choose that way. But the gateway to life is very narrow and difficult and only a few will find it."

Our decisions affect the quality of our earthly lives and, more importantly, our final destination for all eternity. Choose life.

> God does not love us because we are valuable. We are valuable because God loves us.
>
> —Archbishop Fulton J. Sheen

Three Boxes

All of us have heard that we should do some out of the box thinking. I've spent a considerable amount time trying to figure out what that means. I have read about it in books and have had my antennas out hoping to get a transmission from someone who was in the know so it could be both taught and caught.

I have learned about the box mentality and hopefully how to get out of them when it is necessary and beneficial. In retrospect, I can see that understanding the box analogy is essential for the growth and development of every woman's adult life.

The first box is called "what mom and dad always said." Some people are willing to live in this box and consider it's parameters to be the law and gospel for their entire lives. We learn many good things from our parents but quite often there are some liabilities as well. Do you really think that out of the five billion people inhabiting the planet your own two parents could give you all the information you will need to negotiate life?

Janine Hall

I learned some very good things from my parents but I have had to contend with a lot of situations that they never dreamt of. And not all the things we get from our parents are good and useful because they were only human after all. It is job one for us to determine what to keep and what to throw away.

The most influential person in our adult life is our mate. Our extended family, if we are lucky enough to have access to them can give us a lot of useful information that can be used to broaden our horizons. Grandparents, aunts, uncles and cousins, can provide us with some pieces of our puzzle and give us roots. But character is not inherited. We must develop our own integrity and forge our future independently and form our own world view.

Our peers are a huge source of imput in forming our generational mindset and we to some degree are part of the social milieu in which we come of age. Teachers touch everyone's life. And in adulthood, God will send us friends and mentors that will help us evolve. We need to be open enough to recognize them and courageous enough to take them on. It truly takes a village.

The second and smaller box in women's adult box is the "who am I" box. We need to learn to define ourselves as more than the sum of the roles we play. We are an individual with capabilities and characteristics unique unto ourselves. If we put all of our eggs in the "mom basket" and the "wife basket" we may end up resenting them for not turning out as well as we had hoped or for not valuing us as much as we would like after we have done so much for them.

We need hobbies, interests and careers in order to form a separate identity and we all have different personality traits. I enjoy my family but I need other people in my life and special activities and so do they.

If you want to find yourself you need to think for yourself. You'll have to get out of your armchair and participate in life no matter how uncomfortable it seems. Finding out who you are is not for sissies. You'll need to get some of your fur rubbed off and endure some cuts and scrapes. When we state how we feel about things and stand up for our rights it can be uncomfortable but this is how we grow.

Another essential component of finding yourself is some introspection. That is a tall order when the only time some women get to themselves is when they are in the bathroom. A hot bath is a good respite and the bathroom can also double as a telephone booth. We need to schedule time for introspection even if other are tasks go undone.

The last box is a spiritual one. Faith creates a joy that does not depend on outer circumstances. Our wedding day is the second most important day in our lives. The day we accept Jesus Christ is paramount and defines how we are going to spend eternity. We must have the audacity to put God before our husbands and families.

Our secular society gives very few role models who have made their relationship with God as the number one priority in their lives. God chooses us to be the soldiers and saints he wants to work in his kingdom here on earth. Failing to pursue a relationship with Jesus Christ is a tragedy.

Janine Hall

When you are convinced that you know your purpose in life you have to carry it out. You can't show up at the starting line and then refuse to run. God allows trial and error.

As we emerge from this last box we can occasionally feel the wind beneath our wings. Sometimes we can soar. Life still won't be a bowl of cherries but you'll spend a lot less time in the pits because your focus will be on the eternal. We are in the world but not of the world. Jesus Christ is the Bridegroom and He's waiting for you. Come to Him and taste the sweetness of His living waters,

Keep Your Eyes on Jesus

Some say they don't watch the news on TV anymore because it is too depressing. The national debt is astronomical; Washington, DC, is in disarray; ISIS is on the rampage; natural disasters abound; and many families are struggling to put food on the table. And the kicker is that all indications are that we are living in the end times prophesized in the Bible. It's enough to make you want to put your head in the sand and keep it there.

We need strategies that will help us keep afloat in troubled times. We are searching for security and stability psychologically, financially, politically, and spiritually. Broad is the road that leads to destruction and many are those who travel it. It's an easy street.

Just follow the signposts of the secular culture, absorb the thoughts that the media and the entertainment industry present to us, and digest the ideas presented to us by liberal universities, and we will find that Satan has lured us into the ultimate dead end.

Janine Hall

Surrounded by the increased evil of our day and the breakdown of society, we may not even realize that we have lost our way and every day that we live we are closer to a permanent residence in hell eternally separated from God.

God tries everything he knows, short of standing on His head, to get our attention, but often, we humans prefer to think we can make our own way through life without Him. When life serves us a big piece of humble pie, it may be God's way of getting us to realize we sorely need divine guidance.

A boulder appearing in our pathway may be a blessing in disguise because we will need God to provide us with a way around it. Being between a rock and a hard place may bring you to the foot of the cross. Asking God to come into your life is the most monumental decision you can make in determining where you spend the rest of eternity.

Just as we need a GPS system or a map to show us where we are now, where we want to end up, and how to get to our destination when we travel, a guide to help us negotiate modern life is sorely needed. In and of ourselves, we are not wise enough to make our way through the minefields of modern life. But if we turn to God's timeless, infallible word, it will show the way and provide rest and reassurance for our weary souls along our journey in today's world.

Become familiar with the Bible. Spiritual strength from prayer and being in God's presence helps us stay centered in Him and helps our biblical worldview stay intact. Memorizing Bible verses and knowing God's promises keeps us on solid ground. Then all the distressing messages from the outside world lose a great deal of their ability to rattle our cages.

Joyce Meyer has a new devotional book out called *Power Thoughts*. It has a Bible verse and a corresponding short message for every day. These daily power thoughts can help us stay on the right path walking victoriously through the most challenging terrain.

Get right with God. Hebrews 12:2 exhorts us to "Let our eyes fix on Jesus, the author and perfector of our faith."

Christians are in the world but not of the world. Turn off the newscast and meditate on God's word. Let His presence surround you. Christ will never leave you or forsake you. He promises us that and much more.

We All Have Choices

We all need to honestly admit we are what we are today because of the decisions we made in our yesterdays. If we accept that, we will also realize that the decisions we make today will shape our tomorrows.

Proactive people try to make things happen for themselves and others. Reactive people put little effort into life and let things happen to them.

Henry David Thoreau stated, "I know of no more encouraging fact than the unquestionable ability of man to elevate his life by conscious endeavor." God helps those that help themselves.

Proactive people are driven by values that they have selected and internalized, so they aren't overly concerned about what other people think. They are not controlled by popular opinion. Eleanor Roosevelt must have been proactive, because she said, "No one can make you feel inferior without your consent."

Reactive people are sensitive to social weather. When they are treated well, they are comfortable, but they falter in the face of criticism. Reactive individuals are people pleasers and they only feel valuable when someone approves of them. They are driven by feelings and by circumstances, so they are easily controlled by others. Reactive people build their lives around the opinions and wishes of those around them.

A reactive attitude was unfortunately the story of much of my life because of my poor opinion of myself. I was able to change for the better because God came into my life and I became someone—a child of God. He has changed me a little bit at a time. I started trying harder to build a relationship with Jesus Christ, worked through my issues, and began to do things to the best of my ability.

Writing my first book, *Knowing That He Will,* was the most proactive thing I have ever done, and it changed my life. You don't have to write a book to become proactive; you just need to plan ahead, prevent problems you can see coming down the road, and work hard to make good things happen. Proactive people make life a verb, and they are busy trying to improve their circumstances. They are eager and willing to learn.

Just as a perfect set of abs lie beneath sagging muscles and layers of fat, our proactive muscles lay dormant underneath our passivity and years of disuse. Getting back into the habit of flexing them is tough and won't get easier in fifteen minutes, so pace yourself and try to be patient.

You will fall flat on your face if you don't enlist the help of God. He is a lot smarter than us, and He can make things happen for us that are in our best interests if we trust in Him. He also may say no to us when the things we ask for would be detrimental to our well-being, and sometimes He just says, "Not now."

We have only to observe children and young people to see that proactivity is part of everyone's original equipment. When we exercise our proactive muscles by effort that takes us out of our comfort zone, we will strengthen our ability to respond to life and be more likely to take advantage of the opportunities that comes our way.

It's very hard to begin to take little risks, but it's unlikely that we can make much progress without doing so. There will be many times when we will have difficulty in detecting any progress, and there will be setbacks. Rome was not built in a day.

We need to get going and start growing. Judith C. Lechman believes that "no matter what painful experiences we undergo, we must continue to pursue servanthood in a manner that reflects the boldness of Christ." We need to realize that our negative emotions are based on beliefs, and beliefs can be changed.

If we continue to live prayerfully according to Christian truths, in time, we will find still waters and calm seas. Do what you know is right, and you will gain your own approval. God loves the proactive servant.

Reactive people are laid-back and don't put much effort into life. They strive for mediocrity. People who wish to blend into the background often lose their identities. Proactive people do things to the best of their abilities. God is pleased with those who are good stewards of their property and their talents.

In proactive endeavors, we are not so much trying to impress people as we are trying to bloom where we are planted. When we do things for others and for causes we value, we are filling our own buckets of self-esteem if we genuinely intend to be truly helpful for the right reasons. Our greatest desire should be to please God.

When we compete against ourselves, the progress we make will encourage us. Activating the promises of God jump-starts the batteries of proactivity. If we prayerfully seek God's will for our lives, He will guide and direct us. Our confidence lies in Him. Inner resolve, spiritual growth, and quiet realizations always come before changes that will become apparent to others. You've got to build it on the Rock.

Whatever we conceive and believe, we can achieve with the help of God. We have to believe that we can succeed solely because Christ lives in us, and with Him, all things are possible.

If you believe that you are doing God's will, don't cave into pressure put on you by others or quit when you don't get immediate results. Perseverance is a virtue. Go the extra mile.

Sometimes we women relapse into "learned helplessness." I have experienced this in my own life. We truly believe that we can't do things that are well within our capabilities. We bump our heads on the glass ceilings of our own low opinions of ourselves.

We need to give ourselves credit for effort, because effort is in our control and is the precursor of positive results. We need to lower our expectations because then our goals will seem more attainable. There's always room for improvement. Most skills improve with practice. Great things can come from small beginnings.

When I am writing, I am reinventing myself and forging my own identity. If you are a professional, a terrific cook, an artist, or a gracious hostess for the important people in your life, you are altering your self-image, contributing to the larger picture, and making the world a better place. There is a purpose for every life.

The golden goose of personal success is not going to lay an egg of achievement on your doorstep on any given morning. You have to earn it. Because success means different things to many people, there are numerous forms of well-being derived from all kinds of met goals.

If you haven't put much effort into life for a long time, you will feel very uncomfortable and stressed while you are trying to turn over a new leaf. You may have to bear discomfort for a long time to bring about any positive change.

Repeated effort in spite of unpleasant feelings is proactive, and proactive people who persist in spite of difficulties and setbacks will eventually reach higher ground.

People become reactive because they are paralyzed by their own fears. It can take a tremendous amount of courage to act in the face of lengthy periods of inertia, inactivity, or some kind of failure. Enlist the help of God.

God is our greatest resource of power that makes proactivity possible. When we know Him and have access to His grace and power, our lives will change. He can move mountains and make crooked paths straight. Alma Barkman explained how this can happen when she said, "Grace and obedience must go hand in hand or else we become spiritually immobile and unable to move in the direction God would have us to go."

Let's resolve to vow, "I will become proactive, so help me God."

Bad Problems—Good Results

You're not alone if the unfairness and the suffering in this life leave you unconvinced that a God in heaven cares about you. Life is short and full of trouble.

Believing that life should be pleasant and easy sets us up for disappointment and heartache. Almost no one gets through life without a crisis or an obstacle that prevents forward progress. But if we can accept our suffering, we can transcend it.

God allows us to experience suffering when we make poor choices. Just as we recoil after touching a hot stove, our mental pain can alert us that we are headed in the wrong direction and that we need to make some changes, or that we should depend on God instead of our own shortsighted, misguided efforts.

It's My Turn

Strength of character is not forged when everything is going our way, but it is developed by the presence of pressure, temptation, and painful circumstances.

Often, it is necessary for God to allow us to suffer in order to convince us that we cannot get through this life without Him. God disciplines His own in order to get us to submit our will to His failures, and setbacks bring us to our knees.

Without the search for significance, we would never find God. Just as the physically sick need a doctor, the spiritually poor need the rest and relief they find in their faith in God.

The most fortunate people are those who discover through suffering that this life is not all there is. People who have suffered often discover the joy of the Lord and realize why Christ said, "Blessed are those who are poor in spirit for theirs is the kingdom of God" (Matthew 5:5).

We are in the world not of the world. Each new pain makes this life less inviting and the next more appealing. In its own way, the inconveniences and insults of old age pave the way for a graceful departure.

When life becomes difficult and pleasantries are few, it becomes advantageous to lean on God. Once we have exhausted our own arsenal of personal strengths and earthly strongholds that do not bring us peace and joy, God draws us to Himself. We find shelter in His protection, rest in His righteousness, and peace in His presence.

The apostle Paul felt that he would rather be with Christ in suffering than without Christ in good health and optimal circumstances. He asked the Father to remove an undisclosed source of suffering. But the Lord declined, saying, "My grace is sufficient for you for my strength is made perfect in weakness. Therefore most gladly will I boast in my infirmities, that the power of Christ may rest on me. Therefore I take pleasure in infirmities, in reproaches, in needs, in persecutions, and in distresses for Christ's sake for when I am weak then I am strong" (2 Corinthians 12:9–10).

Those who have suffered speak many languages. No one can be more compassionate to others in trouble than those who have suffered themselves.

Because God comforts us, we can comfort others. Widows comfort other widows; cancer patients offer solace to other cancer patients; and as women, we come to grips with the increasing stresses and shared challenges that accompany our gender role in this time of uncertainty. Today's turbulent and tumultuous world assaults the family unit from every side.

The human suffering that is a result of the current recession is apparent to everyone. If we haven't experienced its adverse effects personally, we know someone who has. We see the poignant portrayal of human suffering unfold each day on our television screen.

Hopefully, a positive outcome that could come from recent suffering and unrest is that we learn to help each other and that we experience more bonding and closer relationships. It can be an opportunity to reprioritize our thinking about what is really important in life.

Our deteriorating economy has been a big wake-up call concerning the whole gamut of our spending habits. It can bring out the best in us as we strive to be a part of the solution instead of a part of the problem.

Hurricanes, floods, fires, earthquakes, illnesses, accidents, and riots all have a way of bringing us to our senses. We are reminded of our own mortality and the chaotic condition of this world. We have the realization that we do need God.

In every crisis, there is an opportunity for growth and increased strength, because desperate times call for desperate measures. The greater the expanse of the problem, the greater the measure of confidence and personal security will result when we successfully traverse its gaping proportions.

Suffering comes to everyone, and it can make us better people if we will willingly and cheerfully endure it. Christ's suffering and death has had an unfathomable positive outcome for us here on earth. He redeemed us and made us whole. If we suffer with Christ, we will also share His glory.

Contains ideas from the tract *Ten Reasons to Believe in a God Who Allows Suffering* from RBC Ministries

Tips to Reduce Stress

1) Develop your faith in God. The joy of the Lord is your strength. If you have a relationship with Jesus Christ, you are never alone.
2) Stretch your limits a bit each day. Strive for excellence, NOT perfection.
3) Stop saying negative things to yourself. Quit trying to "fix" other people.
4) Schedule leisure time with family and friends to promote balance in your life.
5) Set goals that you know are attainable if worked at with diligence.
6) Don't book yourself into a crowded schedule. Allow yourself the down time you need.
7) Pat yourself on the back for every achievement. Reward yourself with something that brings you pleasure.
8) Refuse to worry about things you have no control over. Concentrate on what you can do to make a difference. Don't let yourself fall into catastrophizing. Let it go.

9) Enjoy a period of solitude each day to recharge your spirit and reflect on what's happening in your life. A long sudsy bath is a good retreat.
10) Eat three times a day and get proper rest. This is important at any age.
11) Purposely tell yourself "I will do this task tomorrow" and write it down. Doing this can take pressure off of yourself when things get hectic.
12) Take God's advice and learn the art of forgiveness. It will greatly increase your personal peace.
13) Learn to meditate. Recreate a tranquil scene from your past and stay there awhile. Doing so can help you switch gears between work and home or relax you before bedtime.
14) Take small steps toward your goals. Leaping into action in a big way often destroys balance and equilibrium.
15) Do something for someone else every day. Your kindness will be rewarded.
16) Share your thought and concerns with those close to you. It will minimize your fears and you will feel supported. Make sure that God is your closest confidante.
17) Don't put a lot of time and energy into things that are not very important to you.
18) Incorporate several short sessions of deep breathing into your day. It will help to relieve stress.
19) Engage in some type of aerobic exercise three times a week. It is a period of controlled stress that releases anxiety, builds wellness and endurance and enables you to better handle uncontrolled stress.
20) A good sense of humor relieves stress for you and those around you.

21) If you are becoming stressed by a situation, take a break from it. Things will seem more manageable if you do something else for a while.
22) In the course of everyday do something you enjoy. Anything that helps you relax is a plus.
23) Unclutter your life. Simplify mealtime. Learn to delegate.
24) Be responsible for your own feelings. Learn to meet your own needs.

Perfection is attained in slow degrees. It requires the hand of time. Voltaire

Leave each person better and happier than you found them. Mother Teresa

Write On

When you have things to do, it is more likely that you will get them done if you make a list. When someone formalizes a viewpoint on an issue, it seems more credible if it is printed in the newspaper than it does if you merely hear it in passing conversation. If you want to make something more real, write it down.

When it was suggested to me several years ago that journaling was an effective tool for enhancing positive life adjustment, I resisted the idea because I thought that I didn't have time and was not convinced that it would be beneficial to me—but I tried it anyway. I have been journaling for seven years now, and I would recommend it to anyone.

Keeping a journal is a means of making sense of our daily experiences by creating daily snapshots of our lives. If you are very busy and don't always get it done, you will be in the same boat as those that have been doing it for years. Its therapeutic value won't be lost if you miss a day or two or three.

Janine Hall

Journaling is beneficial for a variety of reasons. It is therapeutic for venting emotions, listing accomplishments, measuring personal and spiritual growth, and creating a blueprint for living.

When we write about our emotions, it helps to clarify them. When you get things off your chest and onto the paper, it's easier to see why you are feeling the way you do. This part of your journal is very personal and contains things you may not want to share with others. Journaling helps to pinpoint the problem, and hopefully you can decide what to do about it or just let it go.

Write a letter to someone you are angry with and then don't send it. When you are no longer angry, you can throw it away. This process symbolizes that the situation no longer has power over you and that it is a dead issue. It's also an effective tool for letting go of past hurts. But sometimes a civil letter can clear the air and get communication going, which often resolves the issue, sets boundaries, or creates respect.

Listing all the things you accomplish each day can be a source of self-validation. So much of a woman's successful endeavors are invisible at the end of the day. But when we write them down, we will see that we have cut a wider swathe than we thought. Then we can give ourselves that much-needed mental pat on the back. A long list of accomplishments indicates a productive day.

Every day, identify your "unexpected good" for the day. There will be at least one thing that it a good little surprise every day, no matter how small. Doing this can give us an attitude of positive expectancy that can help us to see there is a bright corner in almost every day and encourage us to lighten up.

Another self-esteem booster is to answer the question: What did I do for someone else today? Doing something for someone else helps us to feel better about ourselves. It can be as simple as exchanging pleasantries with a checker at the grocery store or opening the door for someone. Make it a business to connect with people that you know wherever you go, and see if it will help you feel less alone.

A person who spreads happiness around can't help getting some of it on him- or herself. Do things that deserve applause, and eventually you will get it. Anything you do for someone else will reap a litany of benefits and will always come back to you several times over. You can take this to the bank, because God guarantees it. It is written in the Good Book in several places.

Chronicle the things you did to relax or things you enjoyed. Many would say they don't have time to relax, but experts agree that you actually get more done if you schedule some time to relax or recreate yourself. It will help prevent burnout. Periods of relaxation can bring balance to our lives. An anonymous source supporting this idea tells us that it is not so much the size of our burdens that matters but how we carry them.

Journaling can help us to take off the gray-colored glasses of negativity. If we plug into the promises of God, He can lead us into greener pastures. You can make an entry in your journal entitled "Something God is helping me with is …" Another entry title can be "What did I do today to get closer to my dreams?" My hopes and dreams are to have more time to spend with my family and friends, to deepen my faith, to become a public speaker, and to finish this book.

Janine Hall

In the face of this recession and uncertain times, an appropriate kind of entry could be "What I did to save money or make money each day." Journal entries can help us to define our life experiences. They provide closure to each day and can identify what tasks you will save for tomorrow. Long journal entries indicate a productive day.

The most important conversations are the ones you have with yourself.

Overcoming Failure

Being a godly person is more important than reaching the pinnacle of worldly success. We are not what we do but who we are. God uses setbacks and failures to help us grow spiritually. We learn more from our failures than we do from our successes.

God has many ways of molding and changing us into the people He wants us to be. He often chooses resistance and obstacles as tools to sculpt our psyche and shape our lives. The greater the resistance and the larger the obstacle, the greater the growth will result when we overcome it.

Disappointments, criticism, loneliness, and moral failure are often the means by which we grow strong. He uses these painful experiences as catalysts to change our direction, correct our faults, and strengthen our faith. Sometimes, He has to use desperate measures to get us to submit our will to His and consequently to allow Him be the lover of our souls. He sometimes needs to remind us that He is God and we are not.

Janine Hall

In the Rose Bowl in 1929, a California defensive back recovered a fumble and then scampered sixty-five yards in the wrong direction, which set up the opponents to make an easy score. Our mistakes may not be that obvious to ourselves and others, but we often get off the beaten path or make some wrong-way runs.

There are some things we wish we could redo or undo and many things that we would like to forget. But we can begin anew. Louisa Fletcher Tarkington spoke for all of us when she said, "God allows us to close the door on our past through His grace."

He uses bad experiences to make us better than ever before. He disciplines those He loves. He will hound us, badger us, and heckle us until we give in and accept His leadership.

Shame and humiliation help us to humble ourselves before God and bring us to repentance. An honest admittance of wrongdoing is the first stepping-stone on our way to healing and wholeness. When we confess our sins, we experience God's grace and His ability to make us free a little bit at a time. This is the stuff that miracles are made of. If He can hang the universe on nothing at all, how can we doubt that He can ease our pain and point us into the way we should go?

True repentance or an admission of helplessness invokes a fundamental change in our outlook and our attitude. It is not mere sorrow over our sin. It is a radical reversal in our thinking. God's presence in our lives gives the opportunity to take our weak areas and turn them into strengths, because where we are weak, He is strong. He is like spiritual superglue because He can hold us together after any kind of breakdown

It's My Turn

or crushing blow—although recovery may be on His timetable and not on ours.

You shouldn't think that you are too bad of a person or too much of a failure for God to be interested in. Many of the characters in the Bible did some horrific things, but God chose to use them to work in His kingdom anyway. There have never been many saints inhabiting the earth.

God forgives our sins, counteracts our mistakes, and uses our straying behavior to make us better than ever before. Those who fail are given a deeper understanding of God's grace and love. Scarred souls can help and comfort others who are hurting. As David said, "The sacrifices of God are a broken spirit and a contrite heart, Oh God, you will not despise" (Psalm 51: 17).

In the Rose Bowl game of 1929, the hapless wrong-way runner was sent back into the game by the coach, who told him that the game was only halfway over. What a coach! God is a God of fools and failures and a God of second chances!

What a God!

> Success is just another way of viewing yourself.
>
> —Albert Einstein

Contains information from *David and Manasseh: Overcoming Failure* by David Roper published by RCB Ministries

Your Home as an Art Form

⚜

Even if you feel you haven't got the talent to excel in the visual arts or the patience for hand arts, you can still explore the delights and pleasures of making your home into a canvas that reflects your interests and your personality.

Some people have more aesthetic needs than others. Usually, very visual people are the ones who feel that a thing of beauty is a joy forever, and decorating becomes a priority for them.

The more versatile an accessory is, the better the reason to buy it. It may go with the things you have now or fit into another room when you have the yen to rearrange your possessions, or it might fit with the items you may buy in the future.

Choose accessories that mean something to you, including family heirlooms, gifts, or things you see that you can't live without. Your interests, tastes, and values in life are often reflected in the décor you acquire for your home. Trust your instincts and buy what you like. Make it a form of self-expression.

It's nice to have some contemporary pieces, but don't be a slave to the latest decorating trends. A few well-chosen trendy items can give a room a whole new look, but you will want to incorporate them into your color scheme. Don't buy what others like. If you use buying what you like as your only criteria in choosing your décor, you may eventually achieve your own look.

Many of your decorative pieces are unusual and are heirlooms, gifts, or other well-loved possessions. These things will always be a part of your decorating mix. But some of the items you will need are fairly basic and are needed to compliment your collection and provide that finished look. These generic pieces fill in the spaces and serve as the building blocks of the look you are trying to achieve. A decorating company like Celebrating Home, that specializes in in-home sales, is a good place to look for those complimentary pieces such as mirrors, shelves, sconces, planters, and plaques.

Decorating your kitchen is important. You will want to make it a place of creativity, comfort, and collaboration and not a place of dullness and drudgery. The combination of your kitchen and dining room décor should extend a warm welcome and friendly hospitality to all your guests and help to make your home a place where friendships are born.

Dishes have always been a fascination for women, and they are especially popular at the present time. If you can't find some that you like, you must not be trying very hard.

Janine Hall

Parties, coffee clutches, and everyday visits are good opportunities to grace your table with fun, fashionable dinnerware and food.

Your home is your hideaway and it reflects your presence and personality. It welcomes you home after you've been gone. In my opinion, if a home is not decorated, it is just a piece of property. As Phillip Brooks once said, "Duty makes us do things well, but love makes us do them beautifully." Is it evident that you love your home?

Move Your Muscles

Exercise and strength training can do a great deal to maintain and even improve muscular strength and endurance for seniors. Flexibility and stamina can be extended into late adulthood. The decline and deterioration of the muscles and bones is avoidable, and in some cases, reversible. Physical activity can also improve our physical appearance. All this encouraging news is huge and should rank right up there with face-lifts, senior discounts, and good retirement plans.

The benefits of exercise can be enjoyed into the seventies and beyond. It is also noteworthy that "silver foxes" are more positive in their outlook on life. They are generally the same people who have goals and plans for the future and feel useful and important.

There are many reasons why a sedentary lifestyle is a slippery slope toward decay and decline. Physical activity is an integral part of our general health and well-being. The body, mind, and soul work together to achieve an optimal condition that creates the good life.

So get out of your recliner and move your muscles. The ensuing summary of the benefits of regular exercise are too numerous and compelling to ignore.

In 1997, Chodzko and Zajko listed them as follows:

1. Physiological benefits
    * regulated blood glucose levels
    * improved sleep
    * increased cardiovascular endurance
    * strengthened muscles and bones
    * improved flexibility and balance
    * improved speed of motion

2. Psychological benefits
    * relaxation
    * reduction of stress and anxiety
    * enhanced mood and general well-being
    * cognitive improvements

3. Social benefits
    * formation of new friendships
    * widened social and cultural networks

4. Benefits for society
    * reduced health and social-care costs
    * enhanced productivity

One insurance company, Humana, pays for exercise programs. Physicians have long hypothesized that an ounce of prevention is worth a pound of cure. Just think how many health care dollars we would save if we would take better care of our bodies. A trim, more vital framework is a better temple for the indwelling of the Holy Spirit.

God wants us to be a good steward of everything he gives us, and that includes our physical bodies.

Includes data from the book *Lifespan* by Guy R. LeFrancois

A "Workin"

So few of us get the exercise we need to maintain optimal physical and mental health. As in every area of our life, our choices determine the quality of the experience that unfolds in our daily existence. If we don't find time to exercise , we will have to deal with the consequences.

In our modern day, most people earn a living by sitting at a desk at least eight hours a day and many spend an additional amount of time commuting to and from their place of employment.

In addition, many of us put in some hours at home in our recliners watching television or reading as well as sitting in front of a computer to do tasks, to communicate with others, or to entertain ourselves.

According to a study published in the American Journal of Epidemiology, women who sit for more than six hours each day have a 37% increased risk of premature death. The fact is that physical inactivity negatively impacts our well-being.

Most women know about the risks of a sedentary lifestyle, but find it nearly impossible to carve out some time from their daily routine to get the exercise they need.

Our activities of daily living can be performed in such a manner that they create opportunities for wellness by putting g more physical energy into the routine tasks we all must engage in every day. If we don't have time for a workout, we can have a "workin".

God—Our Greatest Supernatural Resource

We hear from many sources that God planned our lives long before we were born. But we have the free will to accept or reject His plan. Satan has the time and the talent to coax us down the wrong streets and take us to dangerous destinations. If we say no to God and refuse to accept Him as the Lord of our lives, the beautiful plans He has for us collapse and turn to ashes, and Satan will be micromanaging our lives.

Beware of Satan's promise that happiness is derived from unlimited worldly success and social recognition outside the garden of God's grace. Peace and joy are gifts from God to those who search the scriptures and try to keep the commands of God. They were given to help us because they will make life work for us through His favor and blessing.

We can find shelter from the storms of life in God's embrace, where worldly woes and the evil in human hearts cannot reach us. We are covered by the robe of righteousness—we can hide ourselves in Him.

He wants to be a light to our paths and wants to provide us with signposts along the road of our spiritual journey here on earth.

It is literally true that there is no rest for the wicked. Apart from Christ, there is no balm for the guilty conscience. Like clouds obscuring the sky, our feelings of guilt and unworthiness prevent us from coming into the sunshine of God's grace.

Many of us perceive a world of separation, guilt, fear, and unhealed broken relationships. If we would plug into God's supernatural power and become more spiritually grounded, we might be astonished how life would seem to improve. As we begin to be more consistent in Bible study, in prayer, in reading Christian literature, and in spending quiet time with God, we gain understanding. Rarely do lives change overnight, but He is the answer.

We often cannot understand the bitter pills of life. We should be thankful for any experience that brings us to our knees. Problems and predicaments mold our Christian character and fashion our faith. When we feel stressed and overwhelmed, we can run to God and rejuvenate in the oasis of His holiness, His grace, and in His free spirit.

When life turns up the temperature of the hot water we are in, we often try to handle the heat all on our own. When we realize that we could have consulted God, we have an experience similar to the television jingle, "I could have had a V8." We could have God as our copilot at all times if we would let Him board our plane before we lift off the runway in our daily flight through life. What needless pain we bear.

Janine Hall

God is the Good Shepherd, and He knows where to find greener pastures. After all, He is the author of the universe, and He is infinitely more intelligent and creative than we can ever begin to comprehend. He can even fathom our national debt of many trillions of dollars without going into a meltdown. He can change your life in ways you could have never imagined and can initiate a series of remarkable twists and turns into uncharted territory.

Man is limited, but God is not. Man cannot see around the corner, but God has always known the total picture from an eternal perspective. Before time began, He knew you, your purpose, and the date and circumstance of your birth.

Today's New Age philosophers tell us that we all are gods and that we can only love others only to the exact degree that we love ourselves. How are we then to deal with our own unlovable condition? At some level, we all know our own guilt. The answer to this dilemma is found in a divine dissertation called the Holy Bible.

Because God loves us, we love each other. Christ's sacrifice resolves our guilt problem and gives us a relationship with God.

Hope for the poor in spirit is found in the first stanza of this hymn:

My song of love unknown

My Savior's love to me

Love to the loveless shown

That they might lovely be.

That is where love originates—it comes from God, and there is nothing we can do to deserve it. It is a gift and it comes wrapped in a package called Jesus.

Let His Holy Spirit fill you, and sing His praise.

The Least of These

In the Bible, God tells us that if we help and be kind to people that are needy in some way that it is like helping and serving Him. Those who show mercy to others will find mercy themselves.

God has a special place in his heart for those who minister to the needs of others in the midst of their own pain and anxiety. He says about them: "Blessed are the poor in spirit for they will see God." Chronic trials and continuing pain of mind or body keeps us down on our knees and in this way are blessings in disguise. In Acts 20:19a, Paul describes his own lowliness by writing: "I served the Lord with great humility and tears."

Our weaknesses are the perfect opportunity for God to display His strengths. He can work through our deficiencies, and this demonstration of God's power is a convincing testimony to those around us. Seeing our marked improvement resulting from God at work in our lives with their own eyes may be the only Bible some people will ever read.

Happiness occurs when everything is going our way. Joy, on the other hand, is buoyancy that doesn't necessarily depend on our circumstances, and it is contagious. The Bible says that whenever two or three are gathered together in His name, He will be present as well.

Even in our woefully sinful and sorry state, God can use our transparency to reflect the Holy Spirit at work in our lives. If you believe your past is so bad that God could not use you in His kingdom, check out the lives of those God chose to be His own in the Old Testament, and you will begin to feel like a saint.

Remember that God is a lot smarter than us, and He is happy to use the broken to disseminate His message. Sign up to serve in God's army of misfits and ne'er-do-wells. He can use us to shame the proud and the haughty. Second Samuel 22:28 conveys God's attitude toward the humble. It reads, "You save the humble but your eyes are on the haughty to bring them low."

God blesses those who do good things for others who cannot repay them. Doing things for God and not for man produces self-respect. If you exit scenes deserving applause, eventually you will get it, if you are humble enough not to beat your own drum.

Service is the rent we pay for the space we occupy in this world. It's our highest calling, and almost anyone can do it. Psalm 119:130 tells us, "The unfolding of your words give light; it gives understanding to the simple."

Remember the poor widow who gave her last penny to further the kingdom? Christ was more pleased with her offering than with the offerings of the pious Pharisees who made a public show of their more sizable contributions.

David, the psalmist, recorded in Psalm 155:13 that "He will bless those who fear the Lord—small and great alike."

God's name is Emanuel, which means "God with us." God loves the sincere humility in the hearts of the poor and the downtrodden. He hears our prayers and will gather us to His breast and give us peace. We are worth more than many sparrows.

Still Waters

Regular periods of quiet time are absolutely essential for emotional and spiritual growth. In her book *Simple Abundance,* Sarah Ban Breathnach states, "Those of us who don't spend regular time alone to rest and recoup are likely to suffer from what psychologists call the 'privacy deprivation syndrome.'" Symptoms include increasing resentment, mood swings, chronic fatigue, and depression.

The accelerated pace of modern living tends to rob us of natural recovery time, so downtime needs to be scheduled into our daily routines. Take a break from the action by deliberate design to spend time with your family and friends, to do some things you enjoy, to have a quiet time with the Lord, or simply to do nothing at all.

Establishing quiet centers and peaceful habits in areas of our lives can be precious respites to relieve the pressures of the daily grind. Perhaps you meet with a friend for lunch once a week. A tranquil walk in the cool of the morning may awaken your mind and absorb you in the beauty of nature.

Janine Hall

In domestic life, perhaps *Dancing with the Stars* is a timeout in an otherwise busy week. Getting lost in a book or baking something can take you away from the anxieties of our modern world. A long, hot bath can have a calming effect. Sometimes just a change of pace can give you second wind.

A relationship with God has a calming effect, because then you will know that God is in charge of your life and that He has your best interests in mind. Deuteronomy 33:12 says, "Let the beloved of the Lord rest secure in Him, for He shields them all day long." The by-products of being with God, regular times of devotional reading, Bible reading, and prayer are greater peace of mind, emotional security, and a fountain of joy that is not dependent on outer circumstances. Depend on Him, and He will not fail you.

Julie Ackerman Link, a contributor to the publication *Daily Bread*, makes us think when she states, "Some of us may fear what will happen if we sit still and stop working. But something worse happens when we refuse to rest. Without rest we cannot be spiritually or physically healthy. God heals us while we rest."

Peace and joy are not the absence of conflict but the ability to cope with it. God always gives the best to those who leave the choices up to Him.

Even Jesus needed quiet time. In Mark 6:31, He told the disciples, "Come with me by yourselves to a quiet place and get some rest." If Jesus thought it was necessary to go to a quiet place to pray in order to recoup physically, mentally, and spiritually, how much more should we seek His peace in this age of turmoil, bad news, and disasters?

Find your quiet parts. H

Prayer

Prayer, or talking with God, is our highway to heaven. When we humble ourselves before God and approach His throne, we find ourselves in His presence. God wants us to pray about everything.

Marilyn Will Hegelian tells us that "God's purpose for prayer is that He might become known to all men and that we all might be drawn closer to Him."

Prayer is the outcome of knowing God's nature through the scriptures. In prayer, we assimilate more and more of His mind and become more like Him. Prayer is not intended to change God's plan for us but to reveal His plan to us. James 5:13 tells us that "The earnest prayer of a righteous person has great power and produces wonderful results."

Prayer warriors can summon the awesome attention of the Almighty, and prayer is the most loving thing we can do for each other. Praying for others helps us to get beyond ourselves and helps us to put others first.

Janine Hall

Prayer is not intended to change God's mind, but it is a real opportunity to modify our own perspectives. It changes us. Prayer does not prepare us for the greater work—it *is* the greater work. We must make the effort to prayerfully discern what God wills for our lives. Depending on our own resources will get us nowhere fast. Beth Moore intimates that "Without prayer, we return to our own understanding rather than the mastermind of God."

The Lord wants us to pray continuously so He can impart His wisdom to us concerning all the situations that present themselves in our lives. Stormie Omartial suggests that "God is a place of safety you can run to, but it helps is you are running to Him on a daily basis so that you are in familiar territory."

Often, we are uncomfortable in life because we are praying for the wrong things. We pray for nourishing relationships to appear in our lives instead of praying for spiritual growth within ourselves that will attract others in order to have lasting relationships. We pray for better jobs now instead of praying for patience and doing our best in our current jobs so that we might impress our bosses or possibly attract the attention of people in our environment who can provide us with the breaks we need.

We pray to become people of success instead of praying to become people of value who draw sustenance from Jesus Christ. Instead of measuring our worth by worldly success, we should pray for assistance in developing our strengths in order to glorify God.

We need to pray for assistance in developing our strengths in order to glorify God. Often, we pray for our situations to change instead of praying for peace of mind in all circumstances.

Praying for God's will to be done in our lives allows Him to be at work in us. If we learn to commune with God, other people's opinions will lose their power to control us.

Consider the disaster of granting a child's every wish. We are children of God who cannot see the total picture, so we are often disappointed when life circumstances run counter to our prayer requests. When we pray, we need to realize that God knows our needs much better than we do, so we should pray for God's will to be done. When God provides all our needs and not necessarily all our wants, we should learn to be content.

The least stressful and most contented life is one lived in the center of God's will. The psalmist David said in verse 145:18–19 that "The Lord is near to all who call on Him in truth. He fulfills the desires of those who fear Him; He hears their cry and saves them."

This quotation from Ezra Taft illustrates the difference between men's solutions concerning enhancing the human condition and God's way to change lives: "The Lord works from the inside out. The world works from the outside in. The world takes people out of the slums. Christ takes the slums out of the people and then people take themselves out of the slums. The world would shape human behavior but Christ can change human nature."

Approach the throne, and begin the process today.

> Ask and it will be given to you; seek and you will find, knock and it will be opened to you.
>
> —Matthew 7:8

Printed in the United States
By Bookmasters